LEGENDS OF WARFARE
NAVAL

USS Intrepid (CV-11/CVA-11/CVS-11)

From World War II, Korea, and Vietnam to Museum Ship

DAVID DOYLE

SCHIFFER MILITARY

4880 Lower Valley Road • Atglen, PA 19310

Designed by Justin Watkinson
Type set in Impact/Minion Pro/Univers LT Std

ISBN: 978-0-7643-6357-3
Printed in India

Published by Schiffer Publishing, Ltd.
4880 Lower Valley Road
Atglen, PA 19310
Phone: (610) 593-1777; Fax: (610) 593-2002
Email: Info@schifferbooks.com
www.schifferbooks.com

For our complete selection of fine books on this and related subjects, please visit our website at www.schifferbooks.com. You may also write for a free catalog.

Schiffer Publishing's titles are available at special discounts for bulk purchases for sales promotions or premiums. Special editions, including personalized covers, corporate imprints, and excerpts, can be created in large quantities for special needs. For more information, contact the publisher.

We are always looking for people to write books on new and related subjects. If you have an idea for a book, please contact us at proposals@schifferbooks.com.

Acknowledgments

Intrepid's service has spanned from World War II through the space age, and she continues to serve today as a museum. This volume will summarize her career from her construction to her current preservation as a museum.

To create this book required the considerable help of many people and organizations, including Tom Kailbourn, Scott Taylor, Sean Hert, Tracy White, Rich Kolasa, Randy Fagan, and Dana Bell. The help of these friends and colleagues has truly been a blessing while working on this and other projects. Their generous and skillful assistance adds immensely to the quality of these works. Archival resources used include the National Museum of Naval Aviation, the Naval History and Heritage Command, the Naval History Institute, the *Intrepid* Sea, Air & Space Museum, and the National Archives and Records Administration,

I am especially blessed to have the ongoing help of my wonderful wife, Denise, who has scanned thousands of photos and documents for this and numerous other books. Beyond that, she is an ongoing source of support and inspiration.

All photos are from the collections of the US National Archives and Records Administration unless otherwise noted.

Dedication

Contents

For members of her crew, a warship of any size is much like a community. Hundreds or, in the case of carriers and battleships, thousands of men inhabit these vessels. Unlike pilots, who are in their aircraft for hours and then return to ground, or tankers, who most often camp beside their vehicles, the men of a warship live on the ship for weeks or months on end. They work, eat, sleep, and relax within the confines of their vessel. Unlike residents of a village, they can't leave town—the city limits is a thin wire guardrail separating them from the deep blue sea.

It is likely for this reason that rarely do sailors preface their ships' names with the article "the." Just as when you tell someone where you live, you don't preface the town name with "the"—and neither do the sailors. In fact, the US Navy style guide specifically states that the word "the" is NOT to be used before the ship name. Hence, this book is not about "the *Intrepid*" but, rather, is about "*Intrepid*." "*Intrepid*" was a community for her crew, where they lived, worked, and laughed, and where some would die, and this book is dedicated to them.

Introduction

When Japan and Italy withdrew from the Washington Naval Arms Treaty, the previous treaty-imposed limitations on aircraft carrier size, weight, and quantity were lifted. Almost immediately, designers at the Bureau of Ships sought to improve on the previous Yorktown-class design. The result was the Essex-class ship, which was 10 feet wider, 60 feet longer, and almost 8,000 tons heavier than the Yorktown-class ships. The lead ship of the new class, *Essex* (CV-9), was laid down on April 28, 1941, and scheduled for completion in March 1944.

After the US entered World War II, the work moved at a much more urgent pace, and the ship was commissioned on New Year's Eve 1942. Additional duplicates of *Essex*, CV-10 through CV-12, were ordered in June 1940, and they too were accelerated. The keel of *Intrepid* was laid December 1, 1941, on the floor of No. 10 Graving Dock at Newport News Shipbuilding and Drydock Company, Newport News, Virginia.

Traditional ship construction involves the vessel being assembled on building ways, and at launch the hull slides, somewhat dramatically, into the water. By nature, this assembly method has certain limitations, often having to do with the weight of the hull. If there is too much weight, from machinery, armament, etc., there is too much friction and the ship cannot be launched. The less complete a ship is when launched, the longer the fitting-out period.

Building a ship in a graving (dry) dock solves these problems, and in fact if one were so inclined, a ship could be totally completed in the drydock and then merely floated out.

This was essentially the case with *Intrepid*, which was "launched" by flooding the drydock on April 26, 1943, in a 9:15 a.m. ceremony that, due to wartime security concerns, was not open to the public. Because the ship was built in drydock, the launching party was on a small barge, rather than a traditional launching platform.

The ship's sponsor was Helen (Mrs. John Howard) Hoover, wife of VAdm. John H. Hoover (interestingly, Adm. Hoover's sister, Caroline, was the mother of the Doors' lead singer, Jim Morrison). It took Mrs. Hoover three swings to successfully break the traditional bottle of champagne on the bow of the ship.

This was Navy yard chaplain Capt. Clinton A. Neyman's launching prayer:

Almighty God, our Heavenly Father, by whose word were gathered together the waters of the sea, who fashioned man in thine own image and gave into his care thy works and creatures upon the earth, we—thy children, unworthy of thy patience and continuing love—turn to thee at this hour in search of a blessing upon what we do. And we render unto thee our humble thanks that this ship has been fashioned by the skill and strength of hands fortified by love of freedom and justice in hearts groping towards worthiness to be called thy children.

O thou God of earth and sea and sky, bless this our act and graciously guard this vessel here and now committed to the waters of thy boundless deeps. May it serve worthily in the grim but righteous task in which our nation is engaged. Guard and preserve, we pray, the precious lives of those who shall sail herein through the dangers of night and storm and battle; and be pleased to grant, we pray, that no harm may ever come nigh to hurt their souls.

To this petition we add our supplications for the president of the United States, for all here assembled, and for all thy children everywhere, that they may always incline to thy will and walk in thy way. For these things we humbly pray, and forgiveness and light and strength along the way, in the Name of Jesus Christ our Lord. Amen.

Laid down in September 1939 and commissioned in October 1941, USS *Hornet* was the last of the three Yorktown-class aircraft carriers, a class that was limited in tonnage by prewar naval treaties. *Hornet* had a capacity of seventy-two airplanes, a range of 12,500 nautical miles, and a fairly modest antiaircraft artillery suite of eight single 5-inch guns as well as smaller 1.1-inch and .50-caliber machine guns.

The Essex-class aircraft carriers, of which twenty-four were completed, represented a significant leap in almost every respect over the Yorktown class. The Essex-class carriers had greater tonnage, could carry more aircraft (just over 100), enjoyed much greater range (20,000 miles), and had more powerful antiaircraft protection, with four twin 5-inch gun mounts with armored gunhouses, up to eighteen quadruple 40 mm gun mounts, and up to seventy-six 20 mm Oerlikon guns. Depicted here is the lead carrier in the class, USS *Essex* (CV-9), laid down on April 28, 1941, and commissioned on December 31, 1942.

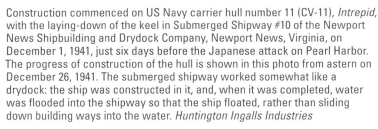

Construction commenced on US Navy carrier hull number 11 (CV-11), *Intrepid*, with the laying-down of the keel in Submerged Shipway #10 of the Newport News Shipbuilding and Drydock Company, Newport News, Virginia, on December 1, 1941, just six days before the Japanese attack on Pearl Harbor. The progress of construction of the hull is shown in this photo from astern on December 26, 1941. The submerged shipway worked somewhat like a drydock: the ship was constructed in it, and, when it was completed, water was flooded into the shipway so that the ship floated, rather than sliding down building ways into the water. *Huntington Ingalls Industries*

In a photo from December 1941, probably taken on or near the same date as the preceding photo, construction of *Intrepid* is viewed from the bow, facing aft. The lateral ribs are the frames, numbered consecutively from the stem to the stern. The steel plates in the foreground are part of the hull called the double bottom. Below the frames, plates will be added to build the shell: the outer skin of the hull. Most of the hull was equipped with a triple bottom, for extra protection from underwater explosions. *Huntington Ingalls Industries*

Immediately after her launch, *Intrepid* was towed to the fitting-out pier. While it was theoretically possible to completely finish the ship in the graving dock, as a practical matter, space and time in that dock was at a premium. *Intrepid* was launched on Monday, April 26, and on Monday, May 10, the keel was laid for USS *Randolph* (CV-15) in the just-vacated graving dock.

But for builder's sea trials, *Intrepid* would remain tied up at the fitting-out pier until 2:00 p.m. on August 16, 1943. At that time, *Intrepid* was commissioned into US naval service, becoming USS *Intrepid*, with Capt. Thomas L. Sprague commanding.

The commissioning ceremony was held on the flight deck, with Assistant Secretary of the Navy Artemus Gates as guest of honor. Following the hoisting of the ensign and commissioning, the reading of orders, and remarks by dignitaries, the crowd moved to the hangar deck for a reception.

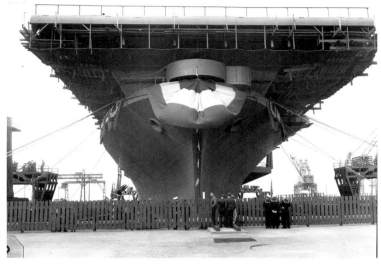

As *Intrepid* nears completion, her hull is viewed from the floor of Submerged Shipway #10, with the bow, painted with numeric draft marks, to the right. Under the hull are keel blocks and cribbing, supporting the entire weight of the carrier. *Huntington Ingalls Industries*

Red, white, and blue bunting is arranged on the front and the sides of the bow of *Intrepid* in preparation for her launching in April 1943. Wooden scaffolding and safety nets are rigged underneath the flight deck, as work continues on the construction of the ship. The large tub on the forecastle is a platform and splinter shield for a quadruple 40 mm antiaircraft gun mount. The smaller tub on its port side is for the Mk. 51 director for the gun mount. A single 40 mm gun mount on the bow was a feature of ten of the Essex-class carriers that had what were called short hulls, or short bows, of which *Intrepid* was one. On short-hull carriers the front of the forecastle was approximately even with the front of the flight deck. *Huntington Ingalls Industries*

Beneath the hull amidships, facing aft, the inboard and outboard starboard propellers and their shafts and struts are in view. The keel blocks are arranged at intervals, with stringers to hold them together in groups. *Huntington Ingalls Industries*

Intrepid is seen from astern in Submerged Shipway #10 on or around launching day. Construction continues on the flight deck, and in the background, on the starboard side of the flight deck, much of the outer structure of the island has been completed. On the fantail are tubs for a quadruple 40 mm gun mount and its director. On the edge of the deck to the sides of these tubs are closed chocks. Short-hull Essex-class carriers had, as built, a single quadruple 40 mm gun mount on the fantail, whereas long-hull carriers had two such mounts on the fantail, as well as two on the forecastle.

The rudder, propellers, stern draft marks, and contours of the strakes, the horizontal tiers of shell plates, are visible in this view of *Intrepid* from below her stern. *Huntington Ingalls Industries*

On launching day, April 26, 1943, *Intrepid*'s sponsor, Mrs. Helen Hoover, *second from left*, poses with members of her christening party in front of the bow of the carrier. She was the wife of VAdm. John Howard Hoover. She is holding the gaily decorated bottle of wine that she will dash against the bow to christen the ship.

The christening party poses on the ceremonial stand in front of the bow of *Intrepid* prior to launching on April 26, 1943. The sponsor, Mrs. Helen Hoover, is fourth from left. Water has already started flowing into the submerged shipway.

Shipyard workers are gathered to the front of the bow of *Intrepid* to witness the launching. Although difficult to discern, the ship's two anchors have been temporarily attached to the starboard side of the hull, in line with the right side of the gantry crane in the left background.

Mrs. Hoover has just smashed the ceremonial bottle of champagne on the bow of *Intrepid* to christen the ship. It took her three attempts before the bottle hit the hull and burst.

In a photo of the launching of *Intrepid* taken above the level of the flight deck, the state of construction of the island as of April 26, 1943, is evident. Between the front of the flight deck and the island is the opening for the forward elevator; the elevator itself is lying to the deck just aft of the opening. The forward superstructure, including the bridge, had taken shape. The tripod foremast yardarm and the smokestack were partially completed.

In a photo taken later on the day of launching of *Intrepid*, the carrier is fully afloat, secured by hawsers on each side, fore and aft, to mules: rail-mounted locomotives that will pull the ship out of the dock and into the channel. The ship is riding well above its waterline. During the fitting-out period to follow, the installation of additional structures and supplies will bring the hull down lower.

This photo was taken a few yards to the left of the preceding photo, on *Intrepid*'s launching day. At the base of the tripod mast, at the top of the forward superstructure, is the conning tower a heavily armored structure with several vision slots visible on it. The conning tower was where the ship was navigated from, and where other vital functions of the ship were controlled during battle.

USS *Intrepid* is under tow from the submerged shipway at Newport News Shipbuilding and Drydock Company to her fitting-out dock, where work on the ship will be completed, leading up to her commissioning.

Around three months after the preceding photo was taken, in July 1943, the twin 5-inch/38-caliber gun mounts have been installed to the front and the rear of the island. Each 5-inch gun mount, whether a single- or a twin-gun mount, was numbered from forward to aft, with those on the right side having odd numbers. Thus, the four twin 5-inch/38-caliber gun mounts, located just forward and aft of the island, were numbered, from the front, 1, 3, 5, and 7. Four radio-antenna masts, which folded down during flight operations, are along the starboard side of the flight deck. *Huntington Ingalls Industries*

USS *Intrepid* (CV-11) Specifications (as built, 1943)

Built by Newport News Shipbuilding and Drydock Company, Newport News, Virginia

Laid down	December 1, 1941
Launched	April 26, 1943
Commissioned	August 16, 1943
Displacement	27,100 tons standard; 36,380 tons full load
Dimensions (waterline)	820' × 93' × 28.5' (full load)
Dimensions (max.)	872' × 147.5'
Armor	4"–2.5" belt; 1.5" hangar and protective deck(s); 4" bulkheads; 1.5" STS (top, side of pilothouse); 2.5" (top) steering gear
Power plant	8 Babcock & Wilcox boilers (565 psi, 850°F); 4 Westinghouse geared steam turbines; 4 shafts; 150,000 shp (design)
Speed (max.)	32.7 knots
Endurance (design)	20,000 nautical miles @ 15 knots
Armament	4 twin and 4 single 5"/38 gun mounts; 8 quad 40 mm / 56 cal. gun mounts; 46 single 20 mm / 70 cal. gun mounts
Aircraft	96
Aviation facilities	1 deck-edge and 2 centerline elevators; 1 flight deck catapult
Crew	2,600+ (ship's company + air wing, as designed)
Decommissioned	April 23, 1947
Recommissioned	September 1, 1955

After SCB-27C + SCB-125

Displacement	30,580 tons standard; 43,060 tons full load
Dimensions (waterline)	820' × 103' × 30'4" (full load)
Dimensions (max.)	880' (894.5' over catapult booms) × 166'10"
Armor	belt replaced by blister with 60 lb. STS
Power plant	unchanged
Speed	30.7 knots
Armament	8 single 5"/38 gun mounts; 5 twin 3"/50 gun mounts
Aircraft	~70 (CVA role), ~50 (CVS role)
Aviation facilities	2 deck-edge and 1 centerline elevators; 2 steam catapults (C 11); 1 hangar deck catapult
Crew	3,525 (ship's company + air wing)

On *Intrepid*'s commissioning day, August 16, 1943, the island is viewed from the front. To the front of the island are twin 5-inch/38-caliber gun mounts #1 and #3, with the rear one higher than the front one, and with lightly armored gunhouses to protect the crews. Above mount #3 are the bridge and the pilothouse. At the top of the superstructure is the forward Mk. 37 director, from which the 5-inch/38-caliber guns were controlled and fired. Mounted on the roof of the director is a Mk. 4 fire-control radar antenna. Above the director is the tripod foremast, which supports an SK "bedspring" surface-search radar antenna.

Three US Navy officers standing to the front of twin 5-inch/38-caliber gun mount #1 are enjoying the scenery as *Intrepid* proceeds from the Newport News Shipbuilding and Drydock Company facility to the Norfolk Navy Yard, Portsmouth, Virginia, for her commissioning ceremony on August 16, 1943. The commissioning ceremony marked the official transfer of the ship to the US Navy, at which time "USS," standing for "United States Ship," was added to the name of the ship.

The aft part of the flight deck of *Intrepid* is viewed from the island on August 16, 1943. Arrestor cables are lying loosely on the deck. At the center is the aft elevator. The cone-shaped features on the galleries to the sides of the flight deck are covers over the 20 mm guns, which are elevated to point straight up.

A ferry boat passes by *Intrepid* on commissioning day. The covered 20 mm guns and the armored gun shields are visible in the two six-gun galleries alongside and below the flight deck. The guns are stowed vertically to ease movement of the crew around the weapons, however, as the Mk. 14 was installed in 1944, the guns had to be stowed horizontally to prevent tumbling the gyros in the new sights when not in use.

Intrepid is viewed off her starboard bow while steaming under her own power in Hampton Roads, Virginia, on August 16, 1943. Four wire antennas for long-range radios are rigged between the two radio masts forward of the island, and to the two radio masts aft of the island.

Intrepid is viewed from straight ahead from just above the water, on August 16, 1943. At this time, the carrier was painted in the Measure 21 camouflage scheme, consisting of Navy Blue (5-N) on all vertical surfaces above the waterline, and metal decks were painted 20-B Deck Blue while the flight deck was finished with 21 Flight Deck Stain.

In a view of the carrier from astern, the two galleries with two 20 mm guns alongside the rear of the flight deck are visible, guns raised and covered. The quadruple 40 mm gun mount and its director tub on the fantail are in view. *Randy Fagan, Floating Drydock.com*

A broadside view taken during the transit of *Intrepid* from Newport News to Portsmouth on her christening day portrays features of the port sides of her island and hull. On the hull below the island and to the sides of the hangar door are guides for the deck-edge elevator. *National Museum of Naval Aviation*

Intrepid is observed from just above the water from port and astern on August 16, 1943. Sponsons, one toward the bow and the other forward of the fantail, each supported two single 5-inch/38-caliber gun mounts. A gallery of two 20 mm guns was on each side of the rear of the flight deck. *Randy Fagan, Floating Drydock.com*

Two tugboats are shoving *Intrepid* toward a dock at the Norfolk Navy Yard on the ship's commissioning day, August 16,1943. Sailors in dress whites are visible around the ship. On the dock aft of the carrier's island is the gigantic #110 hammerhead crane.

Steam is issuing from *Intrepid*'s smokestack as eight towboats nudge her the last few feet to the dock at Norfolk Navy Yard. On the flight deck adjacent to the center of the island is the VIP stand for the commissioning ceremony, decorated with bunting.

With the hammerhead crane looming above the carrier, dignitaries are assembled on the stand during the commissioning ceremony. Along with Capt. Sprague, others present on the stand included Mr. Artemus L. Gates, RAdms. H. F. Leary and Felix Gygax, and Cmdr. R. K. Gates, the ship's executive officer, or XO.

In another view of the commissioning ceremony, the American flag is being hoisted. The aft port strut of the mainmast is to the upper left, and the aft Mk. 37 director, with a Mk. 12 fire-control radar antenna mounted on top of it, is below the American flag.

As seen from aft of and above the flight deck, the commissioning ceremony is underway. All of the commissioning crew were clad in dress whites. The group in mixed clothing at the forward end of the assemblage consisted of civilian attendees.

During the commissioning ceremony, Capt. Thomas L. Sprague, the first commanding officer of USS *Intrepid,* is at the microphone on the stand. To the side is the ship's band, and assembled in the background are officers, Marines, and sailors of *Intrepid*'s original crew, called the "commissioning crew." These crewmen also were referred to as "plankowners."

Officers, civilian guests, and a Marine guard in the left background are gathered on the cavernous hangar deck of USS *Intrepid* shortly after the commissioning ceremony on August 16, 1943. The view is from the forward elevator, facing aft. At the bottom right of the photo can just be seen the track for the hangar deck catapult.

CHAPTER 1
Intrepid Goes to War

On Sunday, August 22, 1943, *Intrepid* entered Dry Dock #4 at Norfolk Navy Yard to have her hull cleaned, remaining there until August 28. She took on provisions in preparation for getting underway until September 14, when she steamed into Chesapeake Bay. Initial testing operations were in these protected waters until October 7, when she steamed for the Gulf of Paria, Trinidad, on her shakedown cruise. On October 16, 1943, Cmdr. A. M. Jackson, who commanded Air Group 8, landed his F6F Hellcat on *Intrepid*, making the first arrested landing aboard the ship.

Intrepid steamed from Trinidad on October 27, returning to Hampton Roads on November 1. On November 25, *Intrepid*, along with escorts, steamed to Rockland, Maine, for speed trials, after which she returned to Norfolk for removal of trial gear.

At last, on December 3, 1943, *Intrepid* steamed for the Pacific. On December 9 she began her westbound transit of the Panama Canal. During that transit, and while under control of the canal pilot, at Empire Reach as she passed through the Gaillard Cut she ran aground while making a left turn. Seeing the impact approaching, engines were ordered full reverse and the anchor was dropped, but the momentum of the 27,100-ton carrier was too great, and she impacted the rocks, tearing a 4-by-4-foot hole in her bow and buckling plates, displacing the forefoot 9 inches to port.

When *Intrepid* reached Balboa, at the western end of the canal, five days were devoted to rigging a temporary patch, after which she steamed to Alameda, arriving December 22. After disembarking her ninety-one aircraft, the next day she moved to Hunters Point, entering Dry Dock #3 for permanent repairs.

With repairs complete, and the air group back aboard, on January 6, 1944, she left California bound for Hawaii. On January 10, *Intrepid* pulled into Pearl Harbor, and there Air Group 8 was replaced aboard *Intrepid* by veteran Air Group 6.

After a few days of familiarization training, on January 16, along with *Cabot* and *Essex*, she steamed for the Marshall Islands to join Task Force 58 in striking Kwajalein Atoll on January 29, 1944. There, Air Group 6 would bomb and strafe Japanese installations ashore. *Intrepid* continued those operations through February 2, then retired to Majuro Lagoon, arriving February 4. Eight days later she got underway, steaming toward Truk as part of Operation Hailstone, arriving February 16. *Intrepid*'s aircraft began launching at 0641 to strike enemy positions. Those twelve fighters were followed by thirteen more fighters, nine torpedo bombers, and twelve bombers at 0719, and a further twelve fighters, eight torpedo bombers, and twelve dive-bombers at 0934. A similar pace was maintained throughout the day, such that 193 sorties were launched that day. While *Intrepid*'s airmen were successful in striking the enemy, the next morning at 0010, the Japanese struck back. As *Intrepid* was making a 15-degree turn to port, a Japanese torpedo bomber carried home an attack, with a torpedo striking *Intrepid* on the starboard side at about frame 194, 15 feet below her waterline. The official action report states, "The rudder was badly bent, the rudder post casting was broken, the steering gear ram room ruptured and open to the sea. The water blast sheared off gun tub #15 at the extreme after end of the gallery walkway. Steering control was taken over by using main engines." No gun aboard *Intrepid*, or any other ship in the formation, fired upon the enemy, since it had been completely undetected.

The blast and subsequent flooding killed three men in the steering-engine room (the machinery that actuates the rudder on a large ship is known as the steering engine), six additional men went missing, and two more died of injuries. Additionally, *Intrepid* took on a 4-degree list and settled 7 feet down by the stern. Even while using the main engines to steer, she was still able to make 25 knots. Transferring of fuel oil corrected the list and trim of the ship.

In addition, the effect of the blast destroyed the landing gear of an SBD on deck, causing the aircraft to collapse on the flight deck. The concussion closed switches controlling the ship's antennas, causing one to raise and thus puncture the fuel tank of another SBD. Also jammed was the aft elevator guardrail, and while trying to free that rail, crewmen accidentally punctured the belly tank of an aircraft on the elevator. Fire hoses were used to wash the gasoline spilling from these aircraft overboard.

When it became apparent that the rudder was jammed to port 6.5 degrees to port and that there had been extensive damage to the steering mechanism, *Intrepid* was first ordered to Eniwetok under her own power. At 1100, funeral services were held for six of *Intrepid*'s crewmen who perished. The next day the orders were changed, ordering *Intrepid* to instead proceed to Majuro Lagoon. Whereas Eniwetok had *Intrepid* steaming directly into the wind, changing to Majuro put the wind off the port bow, and steering control was lost. The ship's island acted as a mainsail, counteracting the steering control provided by the engines. Ultimately, the decision was made that it would not be beneficial to stop either at Majuro or Eniwetok, and *Intrepid* was instead to proceed directly to Pearl Harbor. The aircraft on the flight deck were moved forward of the island, allowing their profile to act as a foresail. This expedient worked for twenty-four hours, when changes in the wind rendered it ineffective. Thereafter the ship's crew fashioned a sail with an area of about 3,000 square feet, which was secured between the forecastle deck and the flight deck. With this in place, it was possible for *Intrepid* to reach Hawaii, making landfall off Oahu at 0530 on February 24. Six tugs assisted her to Berth Baker Two, tying up at 1347. The next day she was moved into Dry Dock #1.

The damaged rudder was removed, the hull was patched, and at 1044 on February 29, *Intrepid* cleared the drydock and, as ordered, an attempt was made to steam to the West Coast, steering only with the engines. However, it was quickly found that *Intrepid* (and indeed all Essex-class carriers) was uncontrollable absent the rudder, with *Intrepid* for a while spinning 360 degrees. The decision was made to attempt to return to Pearl Harbor; however, due to an approaching storm, *Intrepid* was ordered to stay outside the harbor. In an effort to control the aircraft carrier, first one and later a second oceangoing tug were dispatched. The two small vessels were able to hold the carrier through several days of storms, until at last on March 5, 1944, the tugs could assist *Intrepid* back into Pearl Harbor.

She entered drydock again on March 10, where a jury fin and rudder were installed, which were controlled via wire rope from the aft capstan. With this in place, on March 16 *Intrepid* once again made for Hunters Point.

She made landfall off San Francisco at 0612 on March 22, 1944, and at 1745 entered Dry Dock #4 at Hunters Point, where she would remain until May 25, 1944. Although leaving the drydock on that day, she remained in the shipyard undergoing repairs and modifications, including the installation of seven more 40 mm quad mounts, until June 3, when she left the yard for postrepair trials. The next day she returned to Hunters Point, where shipyard personnel resumed work on uncompleted alterations and repairs. On June 6, she moved to Naval Air Station Alameda, where she took on 743 passengers, aircraft, vehicles, and cargo bound for Pearl Harbor, for which she departed on June 9, arriving four days later. During the voyage a reduction gear failed, disabling the number 2 engine. The engine was secured and the shaft was locked to prevent further damage. That same day, June 12, steering control was lost both on the bridge and aft.

Intrepid entered Dry Dock #2 on June 21, where the #2 propeller was removed and the shaft was locked, reducing drag on the vessel. The next day she took aboard Air Group 19 before steaming toward Eniwetok the following afternoon. The carrier, steaming with three propellers, arrived at Eniwetok on June 30. For the next several days *Intrepid* offloaded aircraft, torpedoes, and gasoline before, on July 4, beginning to take on board 551 Army, Navy, and Marine officer and enlisted casualties bound for Pearl Harbor. *Intrepid* began the voyage back to Hawaii at 1702 on Independence Day.

Crossing the International Date Line en route, she arrived at Pearl Harbor on July 11, where her passengers disembarked, and *Intrepid* remained moored until July 22. On that day, she entered Dry Dock #4, remaining there for repair and alterations until July 29.

Among the changes made was to the pilothouse, which was extended 4 feet, 6 inches forward, done by removing the existing forward bulkhead and sections from frame 82 to frame 83. A venturi windshield was also added to the admiral's flag bridge, and SG-1, YJ, and BN radars were installed. Further night flight operation lights and an additional Mk. 51 40 mm director were installed on the starboard side between frames 164 and 165.

Undergoing trials at sea that day, it was found that reduction gear #2 continued to be problematic, now overheating. Accordingly, *Intrepid* returned to Pearl Harbor, mooring at Ford Island, before shifting to berth B-22 for further repairs. With repairs again completed, on August 8 she put to sea once more for trials. The following day she returned to Hawaii, arriving off Pearl Harbor, where she was met by a boat bringing officers and picking up yard personnel who were aboard for the trials, before returning to sea for six days of gunnery and flight training.

After this she returned to Pearl on August 13 for replenishment, before steaming for Eniwetok on August 16, arriving at her

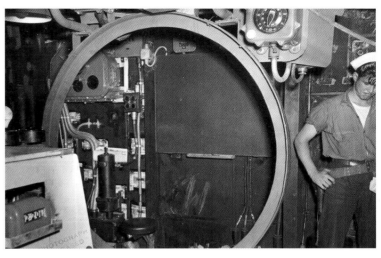

Intrepid was built with a combat information center (CIC), far down in the hull, forward of the machinery spaces, in which personnel gathered and plotted information on the locations of friendly and enemy ships and aircraft in the battle space and transmitted it to the command personnel of the ship, to enable them to make informed decisions. Shown here as part of a series of photos taken on September 8, 1943, to document the CIC is the forward port area of *Intrepid*'s CIC, which was still under construction at the time. To the left is part of the frame of a large vertical plotting screen under assembly.

More of the frame of the vertical plotting screen in the combat information center is depicted. The frame will hold a transparent screen, on which the positions of aircraft and ships will be plotted.

destination on August 24. Until August 26 she operated as a unit of Task Group 58.2, steaming near Eniwetok, returning to that atoll at 1526 on that day. *Intrepid* took aboard bombs, fuel, and aviation gasoline throughout August 27–28 before putting to sea again on August 29 with the newly redesignated Task Group 38.2.

On September 1, an SB2C crashed into the barrier. Seaman First Class J. M. Duren was forced to jump over the side to avoid being hit by the airplane. Despite efforts by other aircraft and two escorting ships, Duren was never seen again, exemplifying the dangers of naval aviation even in noncombat environments.

On September 6 *Intrepid* launched aircraft to attack Japanese artillery and airfields on Peleliu; these operations continued through September 9, when the task group moved to attack Japanese positions on Mindanao, Philippines. On September 12, the target shifted to other Japanese positions on Visayas, Philippines. On September 13, a pilot, Ens. Daniel Weizer, and Photographer's Mate E. J. Ulatowski were lost near Los Negros when their SB2C-3 failed to return from a reconnaissance mission. Ten days later, the men would be returned to *Intrepid* by USS *Dortch* (DD-670), after having spent nine torturous days at sea in a life raft.

Intrepid returned to the waters off Peleliu on September 17 for further strikes in support of the Marines who had landed there two

days prior. On September 24, the problems with shaft 2 returned, this time in the form of bearing issues, which required that the shaft be locked, but combat operations continued. Four days later *Intrepid* and the task group returned to Saipan, where at 0650 *Intrepid* began replenishing her considerably depleted stores of munitions, an operation that through considerable effort was completed by 1530 on September 29, and at 1638 she and Task Group 38.2 got underway bound for Ulithi, arriving at that anchorage on October 1.

Intrepid's stay there was short lived. Because of an approaching typhoon, Task Group 38.2 put to sea. *Intrepid* rode out the storm, her war diary recording that "heavy seas and typhoon weather were experienced with insignificant material damage"; however, she did lose two motor whaleboats that had been left at Ulithi because the seas were too heavy to lift them aboard. When *Intrepid* returned on October 4, there was no sign of the smaller vessels, but fortunately their crews survived.

On October 6, *Intrepid* and Task Group 38.2 stood out for Okinawa, encountering heavy seas en route. On October 10, *Intrepid*'s air group began strikes against Okinawa, and two days later the targets shifted to Japanese airfields on Formosa (Taiwan). Weather over Formosa was bad, causing *Intrepid*'s aviators to "fish around" for their targets, as recorded in the vessel's logs.

In the forward section of Radar Control No. 1 in the CIC, to the left is a radar console, likely for the SK air-search radar. Partly visible on the top left of the console is the preamplifier, below which are the receiver-indicator (*left*) and train-indicator control unit (*right*). Lower down on the console is the master planned-position indicator (PPI), a radar indicator or scope indicating the azimuth and range of aircraft.

Two plotting tables awaiting completion and part of the frame of the vertical plotting screen are in the foreground in a view of the starboard section of the combat information center on September 8, 1943.

Despite this, over 67 tons of ordnance was dropped, with damage being reported to Japanese drydocks, warehouses, railroad facilities, and ships (with two claimed sunk, and ten damaged), and over fifty Japanese aircraft were claimed as destroyed. This came at a cost, since *Intrepid* lost five fighters and six bombers, and, worse, nine pilots and fifteen aircrewmen were lost, plus three men were wounded. *Intrepid*'s aviators continued attacking Japanese positions on Formosa through the fourteenth, with the Japanese harassing the task group almost incessantly,

On October 15, Task Group 38.2 received word that the Japanese had dispatched surface and carrier units to intercept the US forces, setting the stage for what would come to be known as the Battle of Sibuyan Sea, in which *Intrepid* would play a pivotal role. Leading up to this, on October 18 *Intrepid*'s aircraft attacked northern Luzon; two of *Intrepid*'s aviators were wounded, and multiple enemy targets were hit. This was followed by strikes depositing almost 27 tons of ordnance upon enemy targets on Iloilo and the northern Negros on October 21.

The morning of October 24, an *Intrepid* plane spotted Admiral Kurita's flagship and the world's largest battleship, *Yamato*. Two hours later, planes from *Intrepid* and *Cabot* braved intense antiaircraft (AA) fire to begin a daylong attack on Center Force, beginning with a 1027 attack on *Yamato*'s sister ship *Musashi* by eight Helldivers, followed two minutes later by torpedo attacks by *Intrepid*'s Avengers. *Musashi* was under attack by *Intrepid*'s aircraft, joined by aircraft from *Enterprise*, *Essex*, and *Lexington* for much of the day. *Musashi* put up a spirited defense, with *Intrepid*'s diary recording one of her fliers' notes that the flak was "capable of being walked upon." In addition to *Musashi*, *Intrepid*'s aviators reported scoring torpedo and bomb hits on two Kongō-class battleships. *Haruna* and *Kongō* were the only Kongō-class battleships involved in these battles, and both sustained only minor damage from near misses. Badly damaged was the heavy cruiser *Myōkō*, which retired to Borneo via Coron Bay.

The Japanese strategy was to send the powerful surface force, engaged above, to attack the US invasion fleet, while simultaneously sending the nation's remaining aircraft carriers, along with a handful of aircraft, as bait to draw Admiral Halsey's fleet away from the US invasion force, leaving the latter vulnerable to surface attack. Largely, the Japanese strategy worked: *Intrepid* and most of Task Group

This photo and the following one were taken at Norfolk Navy Yard on September 10, 1943, to document *Intrepid*'s radar antennas from the port side. The largest antenna, mounted on the foretop, is the SK air-search antenna. On the platform at the top of the pole mast aft of the SK antenna is the #1 SG surface-search antenna, slightly above and aft of which is the YE homing-beacon antenna. On the pole mast on the near side of the smokestack is the #2 SG antenna, while the SC long-wave radar antenna is on a round platform on the opposite side of the smokestack. At the lower left is the forward Mk. 37 director, with a Mk. 4 fire-control radar antenna on top of it. To the lower right is the aft Mk. 37 director. To the right is one of the navy yard's hammerhead cranes.

38.2, as well as Task Groups 38.3 and 38.4, pursued the Japanese Northern (carrier) Force off the northeastern tip of Luzon.

The Japanese carriers were spotted late in the day of October 24, and aircraft from the light carrier *Independence* (CVL-22) tracked the enemy force through the night. At 0600 on October 25, *Intrepid* launched eight Hellcats, ten Helldivers, and eight Avengers against the Japanese. One of *Intrepid*'s planes got a bomb into light carrier *Zuiho*, and a plane from either *Intrepid* or *San Jacinto* scored with a torpedo in large carrier *Zuikaku*. Ultimately, the US sank all four Japanese aircraft carriers.

The Japanese Center Force pressed its attack, with the US relying on destroyers and escort carriers to turn back the Japanese battleships. Halsey, at last responding to pleas for help, steamed his forces, including *Intrepid*, toward the action off the coast of Samar. The valiant defense put up by the light units led the Japanese to believe they were up against a much more powerful force, so they withdrew. Halsey's carriers got within striking range only

after the Japanese had disengaged. *Intrepid* began launching strike forces at the fleeing Japanese at 0557 on October 26. *Intrepid*'s airmen reported bomb and torpedo hits on Japanese battleships, as well as downing three enemy aircraft, losing seven of their own aircraft in the process, with six of these the result of water landings due to fuel exhaustion.

Intrepid resumed normal operations, taking aboard fuel at sea, as well as replacement aircraft and aviators. On October 29 (local time), *Intrepid* returned to combat when her aircraft attacked Clark Field. As the first of three strikes that day was returning from its target, a group of Japanese aircraft, estimated at fifteen to twenty, were detected 80 miles from *Intrepid* and closing fast. At 1156, General Quarters were sounded, just as *Intrepid*'s planes were landing. At 1204 a Val suicide aircraft, hit by AA, crashed into 20 mm gun tub #10, engulfing it in flames, killing ten and wounding six men. The fire was quickly extinguished, and at 1205, with no more threatening aircraft, ceasefire was sounded, and by 1258 the ship was secured from General Quarters. By 1343, five of the six 20 mm guns in tub 10 had been returned to service. At 1727 the ensign was half-masted as funeral services were held for the dead and they were buried at sea.

About an hour later, as the third strike was being recovered, which included four aircraft from *Cabot* and three from *Hancock*, one of *Hancock*'s bombers crashed on landing, coming to rest upside down and hanging by one wheel from the ill-fated 20 mm tub #10 (destroying one gun) and the forward mast of the after antenna, destroying life lines, floater nets, and a 40 mm director along the way. The gunner crawled out of a hole in the aircraft, while the pilot fell into the sea and was subsequently picked up by a plane guard destroyer.

The remainder of the month was routine operations, which continued until November 3, when *Intrepid* refueled at sea from USS *Caliente* (AO-53) before steaming to a point east of Luzon to launch airstrikes on the Luzon-Bicol area. While the ship's fuel had been replenished, the log of the next day noted, "At the beginning of this day this vessel had only seven days of dry provisions on board. There were no fresh or frozen provisions left."

Intrepid's aircraft began attacking southern Luzon on November 5, launching three strikes and dropping 17.5 tons of bombs, primarily on enemy aviation facilities. This was followed by two more bombing strikes and a fighter sweep the next day, unloading over 15 tons of ordnance. *Intrepid* lost one SB2C-3 when the left wheel locked during takeoff, sending the aircraft into 20 mm gun tub #4, where it caught fire. The crew escaped unharmed, and the fire was quickly extinguished. The Helldiver was stripped of usable parts and jettisoned. *Intrepid* and Task Group 38.2 withdrew from the area on November 6.

The antennas above the island are viewed from the front, with the SK antenna, nicknamed the "bedspring antenna" because of its boxy shape, in the foreground. Behind the lower part of the pole mast for the #2 SG antenna is a steam whistle. To the lower right is the aft part of the flight deck.

On November 7, twenty-five pilots were dispatched via USS *Marshall* (DD-676), who were to fly replacement aircraft from *Cape Esperance* (CVE-88) back to *Intrepid*. *Intrepid* also refueled at sea from USS *Mississinewa* (AO-59) on this day, a task made much more difficult by typhoon conditions that set in, but nevertheless taking on 271,988 gallons of fuel oil and 51,300 gallons of aviation fuel.

At last, on November 8, *Intrepid* steamed toward Ulithi for reprovisioning, en route passing through the edge of a typhoon. Due to the violence of the typhoon, air operations were canceled. Evidence of the storm's force can be seen in a partial list of damage caused to *Intrepid* by the storm, including the catwalk on both port and starboard forecastle being twisted, life rafts and floater nets missing, a cover plate for a paravane sheave carried away, battle ports leaking, the lower longitudinal stringer on the starboard side sheared at frame 27 starboard and frame 25 port, and copper expansion flashing sheared on all expansion joints.

Having weathered the storm and with the weakened structure shored, *Intrepid* steamed into Ulithi Atoll at 1053 on November 9. As the ships of Task Group 38.2 were being reprovisioned, the task group (TG) commander directed that maximum recreation be given to officers and crew as permitted by loading and upkeep. Concerning this operation, *Intrepid*'s war diary of November 11

noted, "Working parties are doing a superhuman job. Have taken aboard in four days stores and provisions which previously had taken from 10 to 12 days to take aboard." It was noted that "at 2330 the last plane was loaded aboard . . . We now need only two torpedo planes (TBM-1C) to complete our plane complement."

On November 12, at last the first recreation party of 289 men and ten officers left the ship for Mogmog Island. The diary noted, "Soon after arrival 37 cases of beer were purchased, and three bottles were distributed to each man." These men returned to *Intrepid* at about 1345, and a second similar-sized group was sent toward the island; unfortunately, when they were within 100 yards of the shore, they were signaled that no more recreation parties were being allowed ashore, and they had to return to *Intrepid*.

The men, however, were able to go ashore at 0830 the following day, and upon their return at 1310 a second party went ashore as well. *Intrepid* was advised that the ship was to be prepared to sortie at 1600 on November 14.

At 0900 on November 14, a final recreation party went ashore, returning at 1145. At 1533, *Intrepid* and Task Group 38.2 got underway at 1,000-yard intervals. At 1633 and 1635, two torpedo bombers landed aboard, bringing *Intrepid*'s air group to full strength, with fifty-four fighters, including two night fighters and two photo fighters, twenty-four bombers and eighteen torpedo planes, and 118 pilots. Ironically, that full strength was maintained for only one day, since a fighter was destroyed in a landing accident following a training flight the next day.

The task group steamed toward Luzon and Mindoro, with *Intrepid*'s aircraft specifically assigned to target airfields at Nielsen, Nichols, Lipa, and Batangas, as well as shipping in Manila Bay. These attacks began on November 19, when two strikes and one fighter sweep were launched, which were reported as successful.

The task group then withdrew, refueled at sea, and returned on Saturday, November 25, to attack a crippled Japanese heavy cruiser reported in the area and two more anchored at Hanton Island off Mindoro, as well as striking Luzon again, launching a fighter sweep at 0620 and, at 0640, the first of three scheduled strikes against aircraft on Luzon airfield and shipping south of Luzon. This time, the Japanese responded forcefully. While several Japanese aircraft were shot down, at 1254 a kamikaze hit *Intrepid*'s flight deck, port side, about frames 130–135. A bomb carried by the Zero pierced the flight deck and exploded in vacant ready room #4, destroying that compartment, demolishing an adjacent compartment, and killing thirty-two men inside it, as well as damaging several others. Flames appeared in the hangar deck, where aircraft were gassed and armed with 20 mm and .50-caliber ammunition. Within one minute, damage control parties began combating the fire, turning on water curtains and sprinklers

USS *Intrepid* is in the channel off Norfolk Navy Yard on September 11, 1943. Antenna masts are raised along the starboard side of the flight deck. The #2 SG antenna and its pole mast are clearly visible to the port side of the island. *US Navy*

As viewed from the rear on September 11, 1943, USS *Intrepid* had an asymmetrical appearance due to the presence of a sponson for two 5-inch/38-caliber guns on the port side and the absence of a sponson in the corresponding location on the starboard side. *US Navy*

in bays 3 and 4, and the ship's fire marshal, Lt. Donald DiMarzo, the Repair 1 officer, and men of Repair 1 began laying out hose on the hangar deck. Topside, Repair 8 and flight deck personnel began combating the fire on the flight deck.

At 1259 another Zero, guns blazing, also began to approach over the stern, deliberately crashing into the flight deck at frame 141. Its bomb, believed, like the first, to be a 500-pounder, penetrated the flight deck and continued forward to frame 107, where it exploded, killing several officers and men, including the Repair 1 officer and most of the men of Repair 1. The fire marshal was missing. Men from belowdeck repair parties arrived and turned on the sprinklers and water curtains in bays 1 and 2. The forward portion of the Japanese airplane, and the pilot's torso, skidded along the flight deck, coming to rest near the bow.

Crewmen began tossing overboard ammunition from gun tubs in the vicinity of the fires, along with the bombs and depth charges hanging from the aircraft in the hangar deck, preventing numerous secondary explosions. Two 5-inch mounts, #5 and #7, had to be abandoned due to heat, and despite constant sprinkling, their ammunition had to be jettisoned.

Gasoline escaping from the aircraft in the hangar deck was afire and floating atop the water, presenting considerable risk of flowing deeper into the ship. Accordingly, a hard starboard turn was executed, causing the ship to list and the flaming fuel to pour over the side of the ship. At 1327, voids were flooded, causing a port list to accomplish the same thing without the need for the severe turn.

Through heroic efforts, by 1442 the fires in the hangar deck were out, and the fires on the gallery deck, the last of the fires, were reported out by 1532. The after portion of the flight deck was unusable, as were elevators 2 and 3, making it impossible for *Intrepid* to conduct flight operations. Accordingly, her aircraft were directed to other carriers of the task group and to ground bases on Leyte. Those landing on other carriers were refueled and sent on to Leyte. The attack destroyed all the aircraft remaining on board *Intrepid* save one, which was flown to *Hancock* on November 27.

On November 26 at 1400, while steaming toward Ulithi, *Intrepid* held funeral services for the fifty-seven men killed in the kamikaze attacks the day before. Additionally, ten men were missing, presumed dead, and eighty-five were wounded.

All of *Intrepid*'s air group, except for four crews whose aircraft were damaged, rejoined the ship safely at Ulithi on November 28. In accordance with orders, the aircraft were left ashore at Ulithi, and the personnel embarked. Orders were issued to unload ammunition and various aviation spares at depots on Ulithi before steaming to Pearl Harbor for repair. Also removed was much of what remained of her radar equipment. It was intended that *Intrepid*'s air group would return to Pearl Harbor with the ship, but on November 29, orders were issued for VF-18, consisting of fifty-five pilots and twenty men, to be transferred to USS *Hancock* (CV-19).

The rear admiral shifted his flag from *Intrepid* to *Lexington* (CV-16), and over eight hundred officers and men came aboard

Intrepid is observed off her port stern on September 11, 1943. Noticeable on the side of the hull just below the hangar deck and on the side of the aft 5-inch gun sponson are pipes for aviation fuel, which were routed on the exterior of the ship to fuel stations on the flight deck and the hangar deck. *US Navy*

from other ships for transportation to Pearl Harbor. Battle damage and the subsequent stripping of the ship left *Intrepid* without aircraft, and also without air search radar. For this reason, it was requested that her sailing be postponed until escort vessels equipped with such radar could be provided. That occurred on December 2, when destroyer escorts *Fair* (DE-35) and *Manlove* (DE-36) were assigned as escort, and at 1630 *Intrepid* got underway for Pearl Harbor via Eniwetok. The two destroyer escorts were detached when the trio arrived at Eniwetok on December 6, and *Intrepid* rested at anchor until the next day with *Canfield* (DE-262), which took up escort duty. *Intrepid* and her entourage reached Ford Island at 1001 on December 13. Over 183,000 gallons of 100-octane aviation gasoline was pumped off *Intrepid* for the naval air station. Also unloaded was what remained of the ship's stores of bombs and ammunition.

Foretelling that *Intrepid* would be steaming on to the United States for repair, five PBYs were loaded aboard right away. Before sailing, these were to be joined by four more PBYs, twenty P-47Ds, eighteen F6F Hellcats, and an OS2U Kingfisher, destined for overhaul, and 204 officer and 1,515 enlisted Navy, Army, Marine, and Coast Guard passengers and ten naval prisoners came aboard for transportation. Also among the cargo were thirty-one bags of registered mail and 341 bags of first-class mail.

Orders were issued that *Intrepid* was to steam unescorted to Alameda to discharge her cargo and passengers and move to the

Navy yard for drydocking, to begin on Christmas Day. At 0735 on December 16, *Intrepid* got underway.

At 1601 on December 20, *Intrepid* tied up at Naval Air Station Alameda, and the next day the first leave parties left the ship, with officers getting ten days plus six days' travel time, and enlisted men getting fifteen days plus six days' travel time. With her cargo unloaded, on December 22 she steamed to Hunters Point. The following day the second leave party, with terms identical that of the first, left the ship. Repair work and approved alterations began on Christmas Eve, with the ship being moved into Dry Dock #3 on January 7. She was in drydock when the first and second leave parties returned, and the third party left on January 12, followed two days later by the fourth leave party. On January 20, 242 new men reported aboard, and on January 24 she left drydock, being moored pier side for ongoing repairs and alterations.

The list of needed repairs was extensive and included the replacement of many damaged plates, repair or replacement of nineteen hangar roller curtains, and structural repair of the flight, hangar, and gallery decks. Also, fabrication of a new elevator platform for the #3 elevator, repair of arresting gear, and repair of the gasoline, air, steam, and fire main and hydraulic lines were undertaken. Naturally, the entire hangar deck was repainted. The #2 elevator was repaired, a new armored hangar conflagration station was constructed, and countless electrical cables were replaced, as was the radar equipment previously removed. All aircraft outriggers were removed, as were the two aft starboard radio masts and the portside aviation oil lubricating system on the flight deck aft of the island. A new 40 mm quad mount was added to her stern.

On February 10, repairs and alterations were suspended and *Intrepid* was made ready for postrepair trials, which began the next day. On February 12, *Intrepid* satisfactorily completed her full power run, and ten aircraft from Air Group 10 landed aboard. It was found that the starboard catapult was inoperable, and that there were problems with the arresting gear and the #3 elevator. The aircraft left the ship the next morning, and *Intrepid* tied up at Naval Air Station Alameda, where she would remain until February 19, taking on fuel, ammunition, aircraft, and stores. While there, shipyard workers arrived daily from Hunters Point to correct the defects and complete the alterations and repairs that had been suspended nine days prior. Air Group 10 came aboard with sixty-six Corsair fighters, a change from the Hellcats carried previously, of which only six—four night fighters and two photoreconnaissance—remained aboard.

She steamed for Pearl Harbor on February 20, sporting a new camouflage scheme and with her flight and hangar decks packed

Intrepid is docked at the Lamberts Point Deperming Station, between Norfolk Navy Yard and Norfolk Navy Base, on September 11, 1943. As built, *Intrepid* had a Type H Mk. IVA with a 73.5-inch run catapult installed on the hangar deck. This catapult could fire in either direction, launching aircraft from the hangar deck to either side of the ship as needed. The starboard end, shown in the raised position when not in use, is the slightly tapered structure at the center of the door to the hangar, forward of and below twin 5-inch/38-caliber gun mount #1. A mobile crash crane and five Moto-Tug tractors are on the forward end of the flight deck.

The starboard side of *Intrepid* is viewed broadside on September 11, 1943. Above the rear of the smokestack is a pole mast, with a platform at the top, yardarms (which aren't visible from this angle), and a gaff for the national ensign.

Tow boats are assisting *Intrepid* on September 11, 1943. From this perspective, it is possible to see the SK antenna on the foretop, the two SG antennas above and to the rear of the SK antenna, the SC air-and-surface search radar antenna on the starboard side of the top of the smokestack, and the YE antenna on a platform jutting from the starboard side of the smokestack.

with a cargo of aircraft and vehicles. She arrived at Pearl Harbor on February 24, and work began unloading the cargo.

Training exercises at sea took place from February 27 through March 1, with *Intrepid* returning to Pearl Harbor at 1500 that day. She steamed for Ulithi at 0759 on March 3 in the company of USS *Guam* (CB-2), plus the carriers *Franklin* and *Bataan* and eight destroyers. They arrived on March 13 and sailed again the next day, with *Intrepid* following flagship *Yorktown* and being followed by *Enterprise* and *Langley* as Task Group 58.4, the ships steaming for Okinawa.

As the force drew near Japan, the enemy began to attack. At 0807 on March 18, a twin-engine aircraft was shot down close aboard by *Intrepid*'s gunners; fragments from the aircraft struck the forward bay, starboard side, causing a fire and damaging the hangar deck curtain. Worse, a 5-inch shell from another ship, targeting this aircraft, instead exploded near *Intrepid*'s fantail, killing one man and wounding forty-four more. The damage to the hangar deck curtain hampered *Intrepid*'s men when it came to servicing the aircraft at night.

March 23 found *Intrepid* and Task Force 58 off Okinawa, with *Intrepid*'s first strike launching at 0621. *Intrepid* continued to operate off Okinawa for several days, launching airstrikes. On March 29, a Japanese aircraft was spotted over the formation, and *Intrepid*'s AA batteries opened fire at 1411, bringing the plane down. Unfortunately, they also brought down two US aircraft as well. *Intrepid* remained off Okinawa other than for moving out for refueling, and continued striking targets until April 16, when she again became the target herself.

At 1327, two suicide planes approached from ahead in rapid succession, both being brought down by AA fire from the formation. A third approached from the stern and suddenly shifted targets, aiming at battleship *Missouri* (BB-63); at 1336, two more kamikazes approached, this time from astern. The first was shot down, but the second pressed home his attack, crashing into the flight deck near the #3 elevator, with its bomb (and engine) plunging on into the hangar deck. There, it blasted a 5-by-5-foot hole in the armored hangar deck, setting fires. About forty aircraft on the hangar deck were ruined either from the blast, from fire, or from salt water being sprayed by the sprinkler system. The #3 elevator, once again, was damaged, this time beyond repair. Above the explosion, the flight deck was bulged about 12 inches. The gallery deck suffered fire and water damage. Two more Japanese aircraft attempted to plunge into the ship but were shot down, one losing its bomb about 75 yards off the starboard quarter, and the other dropping its ordnance just off the port bow. At 1615, *Intrepid* recovered all of her aircraft that had not previously landed on other carriers.

Intrepid was ordered to retire to the refueling area to assess damage and determine whether repairs could be made by the ship's force, or if it would be necessary to steam to Ulithi for repair.

The next day the decision was made to proceed to Ulithi for repair. At 1530 on April 17, eight of *Intrepid*'s men, casualties of the previous day's attack, were buried at sea. Regrettably, an hour and fifteen minutes later, another man succumbed to his wounds, leaving twenty-one wounded. He was buried at sea the next day.

Upon arrival at Ulithi, it was determined that repairs to elevator #3 were beyond the scope of what could be repaired in a forward area, but other repairs could be made over a two-week period, returning the carrier to 80 percent operational status and allowing her to return to combat. Repairs began at 1020 on April 21, and as the repairs were undertaken, the ammunition was replenished. The repairs continued at Ulithi until April 30, when damage to elevator #2 was discovered. In view of this, *Intrepid* was ordered to the rear area for repair; hence the ammunition that had been going aboard now began to be unloaded. On May 2, forty-eight planes were launched for transfer to Carrier Aircraft Service Unit 51. The next day, passengers began coming aboard, including pilots from Carrier Air Group 45 from USS *San Jacinto*. On May 4, *Intrepid* steamed out

An elevated view of *Intrepid* from astern shows the contours of the port side of the flight deck, with a jog in the deck and the deck-edge elevator jutting from it. This is in contrast with the straight edge of the starboard side of the deck.

The radar antennas and the structure of the island are well portrayed in a September 11, 1943, photograph. On a cylindrical foundation to the upper rear of the #3 twin 5-inch/38-caliber gun mount is *Intrepid*'s forward Mk. 49 director, installed at the time the ship went into active service. (An aft Mk. 49 director is visible in the preceding photo, between the rear of the island and 5-inch/38-caliber gun mount #3.) The Mk. 49 was a radar-equipped director for controlling and firing quadruple 40 mm gun mounts. The operator sat in a housing that traversed and elevated as he sighted targets. The radar antenna on the right side of the director has a cover over it. Just aft of the director is a quadruple 40 mm gun mount on a platform to the front of the flag bridge. The next level up is the navigating bridge, which includes the pilothouse. A Mk. 51 director and tub are above the front of the navigating bridge, with a quadruple 40 mm gun mount, the forward air-defense station (the open platform with sailors congregated on it), and the forward Mk. 37 director with Mk. 4 radar on the next levels.

of Ulithi Lagoon bound for Pearl Harbor, tying up there at 1739 on May 11. After three days of unloading ammunition and aviation fuel, *Intrepid* again got underway, bound for California, once again carrying passengers and a cargo of aircraft. She arrived at Naval Air Station Alameda on May 19 and, after unloading passengers, cargo, and ammunition, moved to Hunters Point the next day. On May 23, half of her men left the ship on leave; they would return on June 4, with the other half of the crew going on leave the next day. On May 27, she moved into Dry Dock #4, remaining there until June 8. The shipyard continued the extensive work required to repair the battle damage. Beginning June 12, ammunition and fuel began to be placed aboard, a process that was continued until June 18. On June 22, she returned to Alameda to take on bombs and more ammunition. At the request of the commanding officer, postrepair trials were canceled.

She left Alameda bound for Pearl Harbor on June 29, arriving July 5. Training operations were conducted in Hawaiian waters until July 18, when *Intrepid* returned to Pearl Harbor to replenish aviation gasoline stores and have her radar repaired.

On July 21, *Intrepid* received orders to steam with Task Group 12.3 on July 24; however, that same day, the #3 elevator was found to be inoperative, and it was estimated that repairs would take three to five days, and hence she was removed from the task group.

Finally repaired, on July 31 she steamed for Wake Island, attacking enemy positions there on August 6. That day, *Intrepid* had 193 aircraft launches and 191 recoveries, with the remaining two aircraft, both Helldivers, ditching at sea and their crews being picked up. At 2000 she left the Wake area bound for Eniwetok, arriving at 1726 the next day.

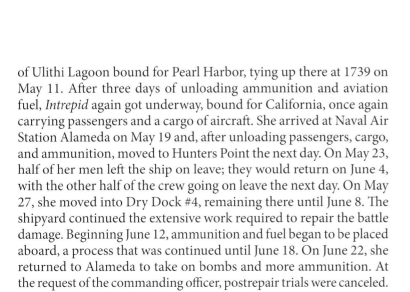

Intrepid is viewed from above and slightly to starboard of the island on September 11, 1943. A temporary marking in the shape of a plan of the hull, presumably as it existed at the waterline, had been painted on the flight deck, and this feature is not present in the photos of the commissioning of the carrier on August 16 but is faintly visible in the previous aerial photos of *Intrepid* on September 11. *National Museum of Naval Aviation*

From September to December 1943, USS *Intrepid* underwent a series of sea trials and shakedown cruises. Here, a Grumman F6F Hellcat piloted by Lt. (j.g.) E. L. Flightner is warming its engine prior to being the first plane to be catapult-launched from the flight deck of *Intrepid*, on September 26, 1943. The V-shaped catapult bridle is underneath the plane.

She was anchored there when President Truman announced the surrender of Japan on August 15. Offensive operations against Japan were ordered to cease. She sailed toward Japan on August 21, arriving off the coast on August 27. On August 30, *Intrepid* dropped her anchor in Buckner Bay, Okinawa. She sailed on September 1 for China, where she launched 102 aircraft in two flights the next day as a show of force over Shanghai, a pageant presented the next day on an even-larger scale over Keijo and Jinsen, Korea. Additional such demonstrations were conducted over Chinese cities during the next two days. Such would remain the routine through October 8, when *Intrepid* steamed for Saipan, arriving on October 14. There, Air Group 10 disembarked and crew from Air Group 14 were embarked before *Intrepid* steamed for Apra Harbor, Guam, later that day, arriving the next day. She remained there until October 21, when she stood out for Tokyo, arriving on October 25.

Intrepid left Japanese waters on December 2, arriving in San Pedro, California, on December 15.

During an October 1943 shakedown cruise in the Gulf of Paria, between Venezuela and Trinidad, four Hellcats from Fighting Squadron 8 are preparing to move into launching position, while two TBF/TBM Avengers at the rear of the flight deck await their turn to advance. The planes were assigned to Carrier Air Group 8 (CVG-8).

Engines running and wings folded, aircraft of CVG-8 are being prepared for takeoff on October 17, 1943. They are a mix of F6F Hellcats, TBF/TBM Avengers, and Curtiss SB2C Helldivers. All are painted in three-color camouflage of Sea Blue, Intermediate Blue, and Insignia White.

During a moment of levity aboard *Intrepid* during a shakedown cruise to South American waters on October 17, 1943, Lt. Eddie Asborne is playing an organ for a group of officers and enlisted men.

A photographer in an aircraft photographed *Intrepid* from an altitude of 150 feet on November 1, 1943. The ship would soon return to Norfolk Navy Yard for her first period of refitting and modernization. *National Museum of Naval Aviation.*

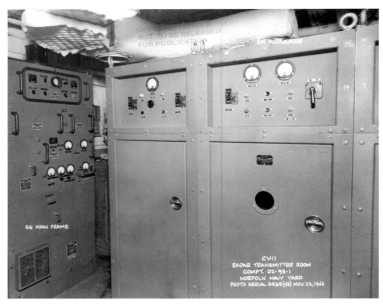

The radar transmitter room, compartment 02-93-1, is shown in a November 23, 1943, photograph. To the left is the main frame for the SG surface-search radar. To the right is the modulator for the newly installed SM radar.

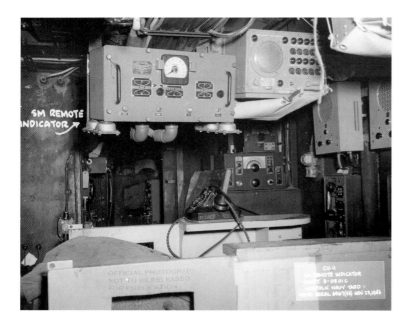

During her refitting at Norfolk Navy Yard in November 1943, among the changes to *Intrepid* was the installation of an SM radar antenna on the forward part of the foretop. This radar was for low-angle search and height finding, for fighter control. This November 23 photo shows a remote indicator for the SM radar mounted on the overhead in compartment B-1501C. It is the unit with the two grab handles on it and includes a height indicator (large gauge at the center), as well as indicators for range, relative bearing, and true bearing.

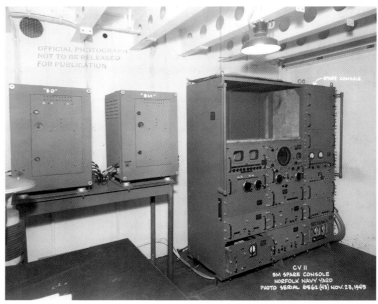

Also taken on November 23 was this photo of a compartment containing a spare console for the SM radar (*to the right*). The boxes to the left labeled "BO" and "BM" evidently are associated with the BO and BM identification, friend or foe (IFF) interrogator sets.

When the SM radar was installed on *Intrepid*, an SM radar room was set up, as shown in this November 23, 1943, photo. On the left are, *top*, an IFF control panel, below which is the power control unit. To the right is a radar console, similar to the one in the left of the preceding photo.

In the aft-starboard corner of the navigating bridge was the radio direction-finder room; the transmitter for the new SM radar was installed in that space, as seen on the left side of this photo. At the center are the handwheel, column, and pulley for training the radio-direction-finder antenna.

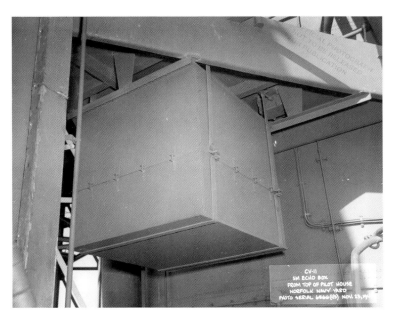

On the exterior of the island of *Intrepid*, on the level above the pilothouse, was this echo box, which was used in testing and adjusting the SM radar set. Above the echo box is a triangular platform on which a magnetic compass was installed.

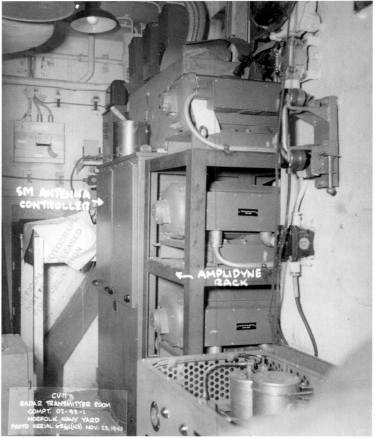

This console contained the motor controller for the SM radar and was located in the radar transmitter room, compartment 02-93-1. Two ammeters and a voltage meter are on the upper part of the console. A placard on the right door reads, "DANGER 440 VOLTS."

In another view of the radar transmitter room, compartment 02-93-1, taken on November 23, 1943, the console to the left of center contained the SM radar antenna controller, while the rack to the right of center held the amplidynes.

CV-11
ANTENNA ARRANGEMENT
NORFOLK NAVY YARD
PHOTO SERIAL 6557(43) NOV. 23. 1943

The antennas on *Intrepid* following the November 1943 modernization are viewed from the starboard side on November 23. The big SK air-search antenna had been moved from the foretop to the platform on the starboard side of the smokestack, and the new SM air-search and height-finder antenna was installed on the forward part of the foretop.

The antennas are viewed from a lower perspective, from the starboard side, at Norfolk Navy Yard on November 23, 1943. The SC antenna had been moved from the platform on the starboard side of the smokestack to a pole mast on the port side of the smokestack. It is visible aft of and beyond the middle of the pole mast on the foretop that supports the SG ground-search and YE homing-beacon antennas.

Although the hammerhead crane in the right background imposes visual clutter on this scene, details of the antennas as of November 23, 1943, are discernible from the port side.

Intrepid is viewed from the starboard side of Norfolk Navy Yard on November 25, 1943. The Mk. 49 directors had been removed from the tubs to the immediate front and rear of the superstructure. Presumably by the time this photo was taken, Mk. 51 directors had been installed in those two tubs. The gallery of three 20 mm antiaircraft guns on the forward end of the second level of the island had been extended forward to accommodate two more 20 mm gun mounts. Indicated at the center of the photo is an interim BM IFF antenna; below and forward of that antenna, the previously illustrated echo box for the SM radar is pointed out. *National Museum of Naval Aviation*

As seen in a photo taken off Norfolk Navy Yard on November 25, 1943, the amidships area of the starboard side of the hull of *Intrepid* presents an uncluttered appearance, punctuated by a number of dark-colored vents and air intakes. The appearance of that area of the hull would change drastically during the next modernization, four months later, when three sponsons for quadruple 40 mm gun mounts would be installed there.

Intrepid transited the Panama Canal en route to the Pacific on December 9, 1943. She is shown passing though locks on the canal. Sailors are crowded along the edges of the flight deck to enjoy the sights.

Following its November 1943 modernizations at Norfolk Navy Yard, *Intrepid* was dispatched to the Pacific. She is seen here with her air group embarked and steaming toward the eastern entrance to the Panama Canal on December 8, 1943. At this time, the mast on the rear of the smokestack remained relatively short, with a round platform on top.

While negotiating a curve in a section of the canal called the Gaillard Cut, *Intrepid* grounded temporarily, causing damage to the hull. This photo of *Intrepid* taken from the island, facing forward, was shot during that incident. Avenger torpedo bombers are spotted on the flight deck, and crewmen are gathered on the forward end of the deck. Temporary repairs were made to the ship at Balboa, in the Canal Zone.

After passing through the Panama Canal, *Intrepid* proceeded north to San Francisco, California. The ship is seen here in San Francisco Bay on December 20, 1943. After disembarking the carrier air group at Naval Air Station Alameda, the carrier crossed the bay to Hunters Point Naval Shipyard, in San Francisco, for a refitting and repairs to the hull that lasted almost two weeks.

Crewmen are receiving Holy Communion during the midnight mass, Christmas 1943, aboard *Intrepid*.

While docked at Hunters Point, members of the crew celebrated their first Christmas aboard *Intrepid,* fashioning this altar and decorations for Christmas services in the hangar.

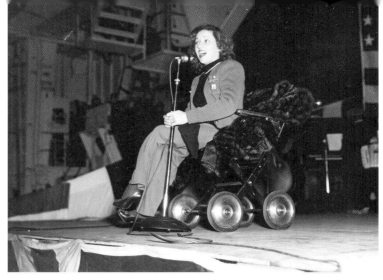

Another performer who entertained the crew of *Intrepid* at San Francisco was Connie Boswell, seen during her January 4, 1944, performance on the carrier. At the time, Boswell was a very popular, nationally renowned singer. She is seated in a wheelchair because she was a victim of polio.

Movie star Mickey Rooney visited the crew of *Intrepid* at San Francisco on December 28, 1943, and sat in on drums during a concert by the ship's band.

Following her repairs and refitting at Hunters Point, *Intrepid* embarked Carrier Air Group 8 at Naval Air Station Alameda on January 5, 1944, and then steamed out of San Francisco Bay, bound for Pearl Harbor. The carrier also transported a number of troops to Pearl Harbor, including these soldiers or Marines who are sleeping on cots under a Curtiss Helldiver in the hangar on January 11.

After a brief stop at Pearl Harbor, *Intrepid* embarked a new carrier air group, CVG-6, replacing CVG-8. The ship departed from Pearl on January 16 with Task Group 58.2, bound for its first combat operation, in the Marshall Islands. During that voyage, the ship crossed the equator, which called for a Neptune party, in which veterans of previous crossings of "the line," called "trusty shellbacks," initiated the "pollywogs" who had never crossed the equator before. On January 22, 1944, "Davy Jones," *right*, and three trusty shellbacks are approaching the flight deck, to be introduced to the captain.

Davy Jones, at the center with the white jacket with skull and crossbones on the back, has been escorted onto the flight deck and is inspecting pollywog officers. The Neptune party proceeded, with pollywogs being hazed and eventually awarded certificates of their hard-earned status as trusty shellbacks.

USS *Intrepid* is steaming with Task Group 58.2 toward the Marshall Islands on January 26, 1944. The carrier's number, "11," is painted on the aft end of the flight deck and is faintly visible. Douglas SBD-5 Dauntless dive-bombers from Bombing Squadron 6 (VB-6) and TBF/TBM Avenger torpedo bombers from VT-6 are spotted on the flight deck. Secured to the aircraft outrigger on the starboard side of the deck, with the Intermediate Blue paint of its folded wing prominent, is a Vought F4U-2 night fighter from Night Fighting Squadron 101, abbreviated VF(N)-101. The radar pod is visible on the front of the wing. At some point since early December, a pole mast had been added to the top of the existing mast atop the round platform on the mast at the rear of the smokestack, and this feature would remain in place until sometime between late March and early September 1944, when visible changes would be made to the mast.

In preparation for raids on Roi and Namur, in Kwajalein Atoll, part of the Marshall Islands, ordnancemen are positioning a 2,000-pound general-purpose bomb under the torpedo bay of an Avenger in the hangar of USS *Intrepid* on January 27, 1944. Chalked on the bomb is "From RA Franco TM3/C USS Intrepid c/o Fleet P.O. San Francisco Calif to Hon. Hirohito, Imperial Palace, Tokyo." The object at the rear of the cowling is a flame dampener over the exhaust.

On January 29, 1944, *Intrepid* delivered its first blow in World War II when its air group struck Japanese forces on Roi and Namur. The photo of the airstrike was photographed from an Avenger from Torpedo Squadron 6. The two islands were joined by a sand spit (*left*); under bombardment is the Japanese airbase on Roi. *National Museum of Naval Aviation*

Members of VF-6 are awaiting a briefing from the unit's commander, Lt. Cmdr. Harry W. Harrison, in the squadron's ready room during the Kwajalein Atoll raids in late January or early February 1944. Presumably Harrison is the pilot in the front row, *second from left*, since "HARRISON" is stenciled on his Mae West life vest.

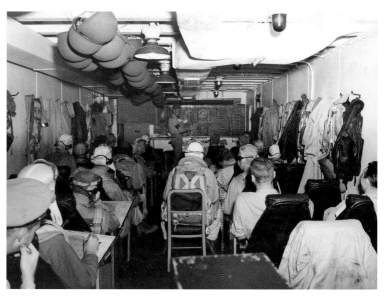

Following the successful first airstrikes on Roi and Namur, *Intrepid*'s air group continued to pound Japanese forces and positions on those islands and on Kwajalein during the next several days. On January 31, 1944, ordnancemen are wheeling bombs on the flight deck of *Intrepid*. The deck-edge elevator is to the right.

Carrier Air Group 6 pilots with their chart boards are receiving a briefing in Ready Room No. 4 in *Intrepid* on February 1, 1944. On that date, the air group launched raids on enemy targets on Roi-Namur and Kwajalein.

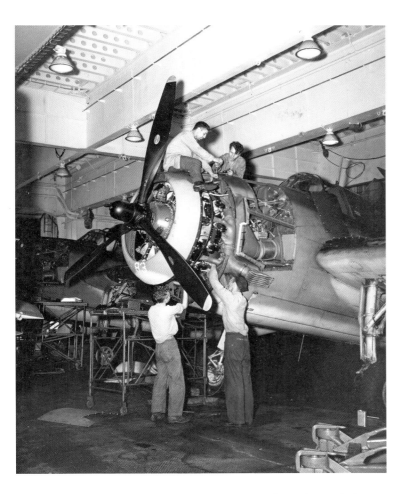

Mechanics are servicing the engine of an Avenger, side number 83, in the hangar of USS *Intrepid* during the Kwajalein raids on February 2, 1944. Another Avenger, cowling removed, is spotted in the background.

Personnel are at work on the signal bridge of *Intrepid* on February 4, 1944. The sailor in the foreground is sitting on the flag bag, a metal bin in which signal flags were stored. Behind him, a chief petty officer, as distinguished by the style of hat insignia, is looking through binoculars, while the man behind him is viewing though a telescope. To his rear is another flag bag, followed by a signalman standing behind a signal-searchlight.

Three crewmen are operating a stationary power hacksaw in the aviation machine shop aboard *Intrepid* on February 3, 1944. They are identified as Chief J. M. Williams and Aviation Structural Mechanics 2nd Class E. L. Wright and D. A. Roberts.

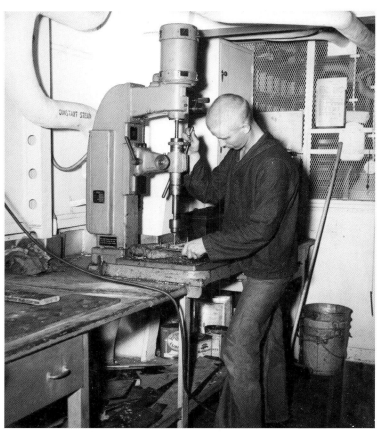

M. C. Halmagren, an aviation structural mechanic, is operating a drill press in the aviation machine shop on February 3, 1944. This shop was critical in maintaining, repairing, and modifying its aircraft.

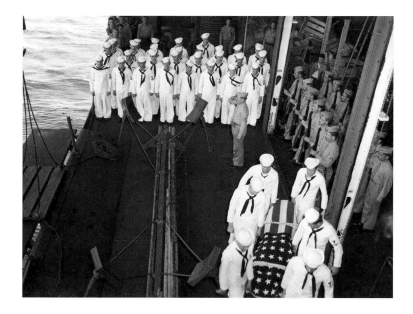

Pallbearers are carrying the flag-draped remains of a member of *Intrepid*'s crew, Electrician's Mate 3rd Class Everett James Eure, for transport from the carrier to the Peyerian Island Cemetery on Majuro Atoll, in the Marshall Islands, on February 9, 1944.

Three crewmen of *Intrepid* are enjoying a break around an upright piano stored on a platform in the hangar on February 7, 1944. The location portrayed in this photo is at the center of the earlier photo of the altar and decorations set up for midnight mass on Christmas 1943, with a bulkhead at frame 58 to the right in this photo. Three pairs of spare 40 mm gun barrels are stored on brackets on the bulkhead, and scores of boxes of .50-caliber ammunition are in the foreground and on the opposite side of the piano.

During raids by *Intrepid*'s air group on the huge Japanese base at Truk, the carrier and her task group were attacked by Japanese torpedo bombers on the night of February 17, 1944. A torpedo struck *Intrepid* on the starboard side, just forward of the rudder post, jamming the rudder and killing eleven crewmen and wounding seventeen. Here, Catholic chaplain Timothy Herlihy at the microphone and a Protestant chaplain behind him are conducting the funeral service for several of the deceased crewmen on February 18.

An elevator on *Intrepid* offers an ideal space for a game of volleyball on February 10, 1944. The oversized sign on the bulkhead served as a warning to crewmen to be ever aware of the danger of spinning propellers.

The funeral service in the hangar on February 18, 1944, is seen from another perspective, with Father Herlihy at the microphone in the center background.

As seen from the rear of the island, facing aft, the shock of the torpedo detonation made the forward-aft radio mast whiplash, puncturing the wing of a neighboring Douglas SBD, which is shown here hung up on the mast.

The torpedo strike on *Intrepid* caused the rudder to jam in a slightly port attitude. Steering was accomplished by varying the engine revolutions, but winds often caused the ship to go off course. To stabilize the control of the carrier, crewmen moved aircraft to the forward end of the flight deck, to create a virtual sail, and they jury-rigged a canvas and netting sail on the forecastle, visible here on the port side of the forecastle, to the left of center, with five crewmen clustered behind it. In the left foreground are the two wildcats, the upper parts of the anchor windlasses, form-fitted to drive the anchor chains. The photo is dated February 20, 1944.

A crewman inspects damage from the torpedo attack of February 17, 1944. The view is looking forward from the fourth deck, a few frames forward of the rudder post, in the section where aircraft engines were stored.

The improvised sail on the port side of the forecastle is at the center, seen from the front. To the left are sheets of plywood, evidently rigged to act as a sail to help control the steering of the disabled carrier.

The damage from the torpedo is viewed from under the stern of *Intrepid* in drydock, showing the rupture in the starboard side of the hull and the damaged rudder. Farther forward are the two inboard propellers.

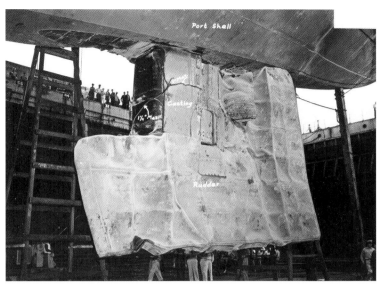

Intrepid arrived at Pearl Harbor for temporary repairs on February 24, 1944, and was placed in drydock. The damaged rudder is seen from the port side. The torpedo blast blew away the keel on the bottom of the hull that had occupied the open space to the upper left of the photo, above the counterbalance on the forward part of the rudder.

The damaged rudder is seen from the starboard side. The torpedo ruptured the hull forward of the rudder post, flooding the steering-engine-ram room and the motor room and destroying the crosshead and rams of the steering gear. Naval technicians decided to remove the rudder and dispatch the carrier to Hunters Point Naval Shipyard, San Francisco, for permanent repairs.

While drydocked at Pearl Harbor or February 27, 1944, a troupe of Hawaiian musicians gave a concert for crewmen on the carrier.

At the center of the photo, USS *Intrepid* is in drydock at Pearl Harbor while undergoing temporary repairs on March 12, 1944. Four days later, the carrier steamed out into the open sea to test its ability to navigate. Even with the assistance of tugboats, *Intrepid* handled poorly. Thus, the ship was sent back to drydock at Pearl Harbor so that a jury (temporary) rudder and keel could be installed on the hull.

As seen in a March 17, 1944, photograph, an emergency steering gear was improvised on the fantail to operate the jury rudder. The rig involved the aft capstan (*left*), blocks, sheaves, and steel cables. In the left background is a 5-inch loading machine, a training device for drilling gun crews on the loading of 5-inch/38-caliber guns. Toward the right are 5-inch practice rounds in storage canisters.

The bracket for a sheave was welded to the deck edge on the port side of the fantail to allow the steering cable to proceed along the side of the hull and down to the jury rudder. A similar bracket for a sheave was welded to the starboard side of the fantail as well.

In a view of part of the jury-rigged steering gear, the markings on the deck served as a rudder-angle indicator, with a scale of 20 degrees to either side of center: the maximum travel of the jury rudder. Presumably the ring on the pin of the shackle above the 0-degree marking served as the "needle" of the indicator.

The jury rudder proved to be adequate during *Intrepid*'s transit from Pearl Harbor to Hunters Point. In a photo taken in drydock at Hunters Point on March 23, 1944, the port side of the rudder cable and the sheave shown in the preceding photo are viewed. After clearing the sheave, the steering cable was routed through a steel pipe, attached to the hull with welded struts; the pipe served as a cable guard. The jury rudder and keel are partially visible through the scaffolding below the hull.

In an astern view of *Intrepid* in drydock at Hunters Point on March 23, 1944, the cable guards for the jury steering cables are visible among the visual clutter of scaffolding and drydock. On the center of the hull, between the propeller-shaft struts, is the rear edge of the temporary rudder. At the top of that edge is a fitting called a gun-tackle purchase, to which the bottom ends of the jury-rudder cables will later be attached. Very faintly visible to the starboard side of the bottom of the sponson for the quadruple 40 mm gun mount are the raised outlines of the ship's name, "INTREPID." This is readily visible only under high magnification.

The full extent of the steel patch on the hull is depicted. The breach in the hull extended from the fourth deck down to the keel, and the interior of the ship in this area was devastated, with machinery, decks, and bulkheads destroyed. The jury rudder and fin, encased in scaffolding, are also in view. This rudder was 100 square feet in size: about 20 percent of the size of the original rudder.

The jury steering cable, sheave, and guard on the starboard side of the stern are depicted in a photo taken on March 23, 1944. Forward of the guard is the steel patch that was welded onto the shell at Pearl Harbor, to cover the breach in the hull from the Japanese torpedo.

The starboard inboard propeller and its shaft and strut are shown in a photo from March 23, 1944, in drydock at Hunters Point. The propellers were numbered from starboard to port; thus, this was propeller #2.

The repairs and modernization of *Intrepid* at Hunters Point lasted from late February to June 4, 1944. The carrier's island is seen from the aft port quarter on March 28. Changes made during this period include expanding space for the fleet admirals aboard, necessitating the removal of the forward 40 mm gun on the island. The mast on the rear of the smokestack had been extended by adding a pole mast to the top of the existing circular platform, and a YJ homing-beacon antenna has been mounted on the top.

While *Intrepid* was undergoing repairs at Hunters Point, movie stars Dick Powell, shown on stage, and Danny Kaye hosted a variety show for members of the crew in the hangar on April 29, 1944. Stored in the background are several spare outer-wing sections.

Following the repairs to the hull and rudder of *Intrepid* at Hunters Point, the carrier is undergoing trials in the Pacific on May 9, 1944, to ensure that the ship is performing correctly. The photo was taken along the front of the island, facing aft, with the rudder at 35 degrees to port and at a speed at 30 knots. List was approximately 15 degrees to port.

Also during *Intrepid*'s period of repairs at Hunters Point, the first wedding ceremony was performed aboard the warship. Radioman 2nd Class James C. Patterson, of *Intrepid*'s crew, holds the wedding cake as his bride, Seaman 1st Class Ann Gargas, of the WAVES, cuts the cake. Performing the wedding ceremony was Cmdr. Donald Kelly, Catholic chaplain from USS *Independence* (CV-22). Both James and Ann Patterson passed away in 2015.

On the same date as the preceding photo was taken, *Intrepid* is in a turn to starboard and is heeling in that direction. The crates on the flight deck apparently were involved in the trials.

As seen in a view from the port side at Hunters Point on May 26, 1944, *Intrepid* had been repainted, from her original Measure 21 (overall Navy Blue) scheme to Measure 32 Design 3A dazzle camouflage. This consisted of patterns of Light Gray (5-L), Ocean Gray (5-O), and Black on vertical surfaces, and Deck Blue (20B). Newly installed features are circled, including a shorter pole mast with an elongated platform on top, mounted on the rear of the smokestack. Seven new quadruple 40 mm gun mounts had been installed: three on the starboard side and four on the port. In this photo, two of these mounts were adjacent to and just aft of the forward bay of the hangar, above the superstructure of the fuel barge lying alongside *Intrepid*. The other two 40 mm mounts on the port side are inside the first and third from aft circles alongside the flight deck. *US Navy*

The spring 1944 modernizations to *Intrepid* included three new quadruple 40 mm gun mounts installed on individual sponsons on the starboard side of the hull, below the island. Since the addition of these sponsons caused the carrier to exceed the width of the locks of the Panama Canal, the sponsons were designed to be removed temporarily, along with their gun mounts, prior to passage through the canal. Circled above the rear of the smokestack is the new platform, equipped with a YJ antenna, with an SG surface-search antenna yet to be installed there. The circles on the island denote Mk. 51 directors for the new quad 40s below. Above the front of the smokestack, the foretop has been extended to the rear to support an SK antenna. *Randy Fagan, Floating Drydock.com*

The starboard side of *Intrepid* is observed from aft of her island. Embarked on the flight deck were a number of Lockheed PV-1 Ventura patrol bombers, evidently to be ferried to the ship's next destination, Pearl Harbor. *Randy Fagan, Floating Drydock.com*

Lockheed Venturas are spotted on the aft part of the flight deck of *Intrepid* at Hunters Point. On the starboard side of the Ventura, to the rear, is the aft antenna mast, partially lowered. At the foot of the mast is a platform and a guard cage, which tilted in unison with the antenna. On a platform above the fantail are six stowed smoke tanks, for laying down smokescreens. *Randy Fagan, Floating Drydock.com*

In a final view of *Intrepid* at Hunters Point in early June 1944, the application of Light Gray paint on the framing on the underside of the flight deck is evident. Grumman F6F Hellcats with covers over the cowlings are spotted on the front of the flight deck. *Randy Fagan, Floating Drydock.com*

In a view from the port side of the smokestack of *Intrepid*, facing aft, before the deck cargo was loaded, visible at left are a horn and the fire-control radar antenna atop the aft Mk. 37 director. Indicated by circles and lines above the port side of the ship are newly installed features, including several quadruple 40 mm gun mounts. *Randy Fagan, Floating Drydock.com*

A May 26, 1944, view from the island of *Intrepid*, facing forward, shows the port side of the air-defense platform and the Mk. 37 director and its foundation in the foreground, and a quadruple 40 mm gun mount to the front. To the left on the platform is a sky-lookout chair, which was equipped with a seat for an observer, a yoke to hold binoculars, and elevation and azimuth indicators. The seat and yoke swiveled to allow the observer to freely search the sky. On the splinter shield adjacent to the chair is an aircraft recognition chart. To the right front of the chair is a target designator, which, when equipped with binoculars on top, allowed the operator to acquire incoming enemy aircraft and transmit information on the location and path of the target to the directors.

The following series of photos of *Intrepid* underway off Hunters Point are dated June 2, 1944. The date may be off by one day: the carrier's war diary indicates that she was docked at berths 10 and 11 at Hunters Point on June 2, but that she departed from her berths on June 3 for more postrepair trials in the Pacific off San Francisco. Thus, perhaps these photos actually were taken on June 3. *US Navy*

Intrepid is viewed from dead ahead off Hunters Point. The two forward antenna masts were partially tilted outward. *US Navy*

A tugboat accompanies *Intrepid* in a view taken just off her starboard bow, 45 degrees off her centerline. The folded right wings of aircraft on the flight deck form what appears to be an uninterrupted, tilted structure above the starboard side of the deck. *US Navy*

The overall design of the Measure 32/3D camouflage on the port side of *Intrepid* is visible in another early June 1944 view. *US Navy*

In an aerial view presumably taken on the same date as the preceding several photos, a wide variety of aircraft and vehicles are tightly spotted on the flight deck. On the aft end of the deck are several Northrop P-61 night fighters, to the front of which are some Lockheed Venturas. Aft of and alongside the island are numerous cargo trucks of different types. Several land-based observation and utility aircraft are opposite the forward part of the island. On the front part of the flight deck are Grumman F6Fs, amid which are what appear to be Douglas SBD Dauntless dive-bombers.

In another aerial view from above *Intrepid*'s aft-port quarter, the same agglomeration of aircraft and trucks seen in the preceding photo is present. The outer wing sections of the P-61s near the rear of the flight deck have been removed for transport. Small trucks are parked at the rear of the deck. The war diary of *Intrepid* does not mention the embarking of these planes and trucks, but obviously the carrier was going to ferry them to another port.

With *Intrepid* back at sea off Pearl Harbor on July 29, 1944, members of the crew are assembled on the flight deck to watch a demonstration of a radio-controlled Radioplane TDD target drone. These drones would be launched from the ship, and the antiaircraft gun crews would try to shoot them down. Another method of conducting antiaircraft target practice was for a plane to tow a target streamer, which could be dangerous to the pilot of the aircraft.

In the forward part of the island, as revamped in the spring of 1944 and photographed in August 1944, the quadruple 40 mm gun mount, platform, and splinter shield that was to the lower front of the navigating bridge had been removed, and the bridge has been extended forward and fitted with a glass windscreen.

Some of *Intrepid*'s Measure 32/3A camouflage scheme is visible in this aerial photo of the ship cruising in the Pacific on September 4, 1944, while en route to the Palau Islands. With the low sun reflecting off the starboard side of the ship, the Light Gray and Ocean Gray areas are difficult to differentiate. The platform on top of the recently installed pole mast on the rear of the smokestack was teardrop shaped, as seen from above. Significantly, the quadruple 40 mm gun mount on the starboard side of the hangar deck at frame 160 had been reemplaced on a sponson at that location, to give those guns an enlarged field of fire. This feature is visible as a dark-colored mass on the side of the hull, midway between the rear of the island and the stern. *National Museum of Naval Aviation*

In October 1944, *Intrepid*'s air group, CVG-18, participated in a series of raids on Japanese forces on Okinawa, Formosa, and the Philippine Islands, in order to preempt enemy reinforcement of its troops in the Philippines, soon to be invaded by US forces. Here, aircraft from *Intrepid* are attacking an unidentified Japanese aircraft carrier on October 18, 1944. There is no record of any Japanese carriers having been sunk in October 16, 1944 until on the twenty-fifth, in the Battle of Leyte Gulf.

USS *Intrepid*, operating with Task Group 38.2, played a key role in the Battle of Leyte Gulf, the largest naval battle of World War II and perhaps of the history of the world. Among other things, *Intrepid*'s Carrier Air Group 18 was instrumental of the sinking of the Japanese Yamato-class battleship *Musashi* on the second day of the battle, October 24, 1944. In this photo, taken from the rear-seat crewman of an aircraft from Intrepid, a Curtiss SB2C-3 Helldiver from VB-18, is being launched from the carrier on the day of *Musashi*'s sinking.

On the afternoon of October 29, 1944, on a day that aircraft from *Intrepid* and Task Group 38.2 were attacking Japanese forces around Manila, Japanese kamikaze planes attacked the task group. One of them crashed into a gallery of 20 mm guns on the port side of the flight deck of *Intrepid,* causing a fire, destroying several of the gun mounts, and killing ten crewmen and wounding up to ten (accounts of the number of wounded vary). A photographer standing behind an Avenger on USS *Cabot* (CVL-28) photographed the attack on *Intrepid*.

The 20 mm gun gallery struck by the kamikaze plane, referred to as tub 10, is in flames. On the flight deck to the side of the gun gallery are several barrier posts, which held wires that would stop an out-of-control aircraft upon landing. These posts were hinged, and they folded down flush onto the flight deck when not in use.

Crewmen of *Intrepid* are cleaning up tub 10 following the Japanese kamikaze strike on October 29, 1944. The second 20 mm gun from the left took a hit from the Japanese plane, bending down the barrel and the armored shield.

Deck crewmen are extinguishing the fire in tub 10 on the afternoon of October 29, 1944. These guns had been manned by black stewards' mates.

The same bent-barreled 20 mm gun seen in the preceding photo is seen from another perspective during cleanup operations on October 29, 1944. The impact of the kamikaze plane split open the splinter shield next to the kneeling sailor at the center of the photo.

From this perspective, it becomes clear that the SB2C-3 from USS *Hancock* was hung up on the second-from-rear radio mast. The gunner of the aircraft climbed out through the large gash visible on the underside of the fuselage. The aft mast is partly visible in the background, above the forward end of the Helldiver's open bomb-bay doors. *Naval History and Heritage Command*

Intrepid crewmen are conducting and witnessing the burial-at-sea service for nine of their fallen comrades who were killed in action at their 20 mm guns in tub 10 on October 29, 1944.

One day after *Intrepid*'s first kamikaze attack, the carrier suffered another mishap, when a Curtiss SB2C-3 Helldiver from USS *Hancock* (CV-19) ran off the flight deck during a nighttime landing and became hung up in the aft radio mast. *Naval History and Heritage Command*

Upon landing on *Intrepid* on November 3, 1944, a SB2C Helldiver, side number 53, veered off the flight deck, its nose coming to rest on the starboard catwalk between the two forward antenna masts. To the far left, a mobile crash crane is approaching to assist in extricating the Helldiver.

USS *Intrepid* retired from her station off the Philippines in early November 1944, reporting to Ulithi, in the Caroline Islands, to take on supplies and allow her crew rest and recreation. Among the materiel taken aboard at Ulithi was this SB2C Helldiver, which the aircraft crane is hoisting from a landing craft tank (LCT). This crane was the forward one on the starboard side. At the upper left is the gun house of twin 5-inch/38-caliber gun mount #1, with hood for the trainer's telescope jutting from its side.

Two landing craft are delivering boxes of supplies to *Intrepid* during a nighttime operation on November 12, 1944. The boxes are loaded in cargo nets, which a crane will hoist aboard. The base of the crane is to the right of center; it is just outside and aft of the rear starboard hangar door. The platform over the edge of the hull that the sailors are standing on replaced *Intrepid*'s hangar catapult extensions during refit.

Supplies are stacked in *Intrepid*'s hangar just aft of elevator #3, sharing space with a TBF/TBM Avenger torpedo bomber, during the nighttime resupply operation on November 12, 1944. The elevator track is just visible at the far left. Many if not all of the boxes in the foreground contain canned tomatoes.

Kamikaze planes again attacked USS *Intrepid* and other ships in her mate in the task group, including USS *Hancock* (CV-19), on the afternoon of November 25, 1944, off the Philippines. Gunners in a 20 mm gun gallery on the starboard side aft of twin 5-inch/38-caliber gun #7 are looking astern, as flak bursts erupt not far above the water as USN gunners attempt to shoot down the low-flying enemy planes with 5-inch/38-caliber dual-purpose guns.

Around the same time the preceding photo was taken, gunners in a 20 mm gun gallery are firing at incoming Japanese suicide planes off the starboard beam. Jets of water are shooting up to the far left, where 20 mm projectiles are striking the water. Both of the forward twin 5-inch/38-caliber guns are trained almost forward, ready to meet threats to the front.

A Japanese kamikaze aircraft, reported by crewmen to have been a Mitsubishi A6M Zero, is on fire moments before crashing onto the flight deck of *Intrepid* on November 25, 1944.

Crewmen of quadruple 40 mm guns on USS *New Jersey* (BB-62) watch as a ball of flame and smoke boil up from *Intrepid* in the center background, after being struck by a kamikaze plane. The view of the carrier is from the front.

Flames erupt on the flight deck of *Intrepid* as a Japanese suicide plane crashes aft of the island on November 25. A photographer snapped the photo from the starboard catwalk, with the island in the right background. Upon the plane's impact with the flight deck, a bomb it was carrying crashed through that deck, exploding below in ready room #4. Nobody was in that compartment at the time, but thirty-two crewmen in an adjoining compartment were killed.

A photographer in the port catwalk of *Intrepid* captured this view of smoke and flames roaring upward in the immediate aftermath of the kamikaze strike on November 25, 1944. Visible toward the upper left is the foremast.

Flak bursts are peppering the sky in the distance as fire and flames pour out of the breaches in the hull of *Intrepid*. The view is from the forward part of the port catwalk, with single 5-inch/38-caliber gun mounts #2 and #4 in the foreground. The object in the lower right is a drop tank in one of the floater net baskets in preparation for installation on one of *Intrepid*'s aircraft following recovery.

Intrepid is engulfed in thick smoke, as seen from USS *Iowa* (BB-61) on November 25, 1944. The view is from the forward starboard quarter of the carrier. Another photo exists of the stricken carrier at approximately the same moment, except from the port quarter, and it is clear that nearly the entire carrier except for the extreme forward part of the bow and flight deck was engulfed in smoke at this time. *National Museum of Naval Aviation*

After the kamikaze attack on November 26, 1944, firefighters on the flight deck of *Intrepid* are working to put out the fires there. What looks at first glance to be a wrecked aircraft on the deck in the background is actually a section of flight deck that was blown upward from the blast.

The same area of flight deck seen in the preceding photo is viewed from up in the island, facing aft. At the center is the section of flight deck that was blown upward. Smoke is still issuing out of the hole in the deck there, and the firefighters are spraying water down through the hole into the gallery deck and the hangar.

Crewmen are handling fire hoses on the forward part of the flight deck, with the island looming in the background. Smoke continues to roil up thickly from the after flight deck.

The crewmen spraying water into the hole in the flight deck following the November 25 kamikaze attack are seen from the port catwalk, with the deck-edge elevator to the right. Fire hoses were coupled to any available hydrant.

On the starboard catwalk and the flight deck, far to the front of the island, crewmen are running fire hoses from hydrants to the scene of the fires farther aft. It took the crew several hours to get the fires under control. Casualties from the November 25, 1944, kamikaze attack totaled sixty-nine killed and thirty-five wounded.

In the aftermath of the November 25 kamikaze attack, personnel of *Intrepid* are attempting temporary repairs on the portion of the flight deck where a suicide plane crashed. In the foreground, a sailor is cutting the bulged deck with a torch. Damage to the ship was extensive, forcing her to leave the area of operations around the Philippines and travel to Hunters Point Naval Shipyard, California, for permanent repairs.

USS *Intrepid* arrived at Hunters Point, San Francisco, on December 20, 1944, and repairs to the damage caused by the November 25 kamikaze attack began. By now, *Intrepid* had spent so much time at Hunters Point for repairs and refittings (three times in the previous twelve months) that the shipyard workers started referring to her as "our ship." In a photo taken in late December 1944, workers have stripped away temporary repairs to the flight deck, in preparation to repairing the deck and the damaged compartments below.

In addition to repairs to torpedo damage to *Intrepid,* during her period at Hunters Point in early 1945, the carrier also underwent modernization. She was fitted with a new quadruple 40 mm gun mount on the fantail, an enlarged sponson to accommodate both 40 mm mounts on the fantail, Mk. 12/22 fire-control radar antennas to replace the Mk. 4 antennas on the 5-inch gun directors, and other changes. In this view off the port bow in San Francisco Bay on February 20, 1945, the new Mk. 12/22 antennas are circled to the front and the rear of the island. The starboard anchor is visible just above the surface of the water. *US Navy*

In a view of *Intrepid* from port on February 20, 1945, the new Mk. 22/12 antennas and the new sponson on the stern are circled. Embarked on *Intrepid* at this time was her new air group, CVG-10, which consisted of thirty Corsairs, fifteen Helldivers, and fifteen Avengers. Also embarked for ferrying were aircraft of Carrier Air Group 88 and Lockheed PV-2 Harpoons of Patrol Bombing Squadron 142 (VPB-142). *US Navy*

The new sponson on the stern, circled toward the right, supported two quadruple 40 mm gun mounts, their splinter shields, and, between the two mounts, two new, cylindrical director towers, with two Mk. 51 directors, the aft one of which was several feet lower than the forward one. At this time the carrier had a total of seventeen quadruple 40 mm gun mounts and seventy-six 20 mm antiaircraft guns, including thirty-eight single Mk. 4s and nineteen twin Mk. 24s. *National Museum of Naval Aviation*

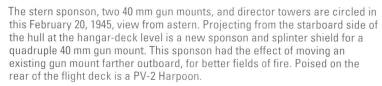

The stern sponson, two 40 mm gun mounts, and director towers are circled in this February 20, 1945, view from astern. Projecting from the starboard side of the hull at the hangar-deck level is a new sponson and splinter shield for a quadruple 40 mm gun mount. This sponson had the effect of moving an existing gun mount farther outboard, for better fields of fire. Poised on the rear of the flight deck is a PV-2 Harpoon.

Intrepid presents her port bow in San Francisco Bay on February 20, 1945. From this perspective, there were no noticeable changes to the hull compared with a photo from a similar perspective earlier in this book, dated June 2, 1944. *US Navy*

Intrepid is viewed from forward in an aerial photo taken in San Francisco Bay on February 20, 1945. On this date, she departed from San Francisco for Pearl Harbor, with aircraft of Carrier Air Groups 10 and 88 and Patrol Bombing Squadron 142 embarked. *Randy Fagan, Floating Drydock.com*

Moments within the taking of the preceding aerial view, the photographer snapped this one of *Intrepid* from off her port stern. More details are visible of the additional quad 40 mm gun mount on the fantail, and the new, cylindrical towers for the two Mk. 51 directors between the 40 mm gun mounts on the fantail. *Randy Fagan, Floating Drydock.com*

As viewed from an aircraft flying off *Intrepid*'s starboard bow, the carrier is proceeding in San Francisco Bay on the date of her departure for Pearl Harbor, February 20, 1945. During her recent repairs and modernization at Hunters Point, *Intrepid* had received her final camouflage scheme of World War II: Measure 22, consisting of Navy Blue (5-N) on the hull from the waterline up to the hangar deck, and Haze Gray (5-H) on all vertical surfaces above the hangar deck. The new camouflage scheme appears to good effect in this photo. *US Navy*

A tugboat escorts USS *Intrepid* in this final photo of the carrier departing from San Francisco Bay on February 20, 1945. It is readily apparent how the two 40 mm gun sponsons jutting from the hangar deck improved the fields of fire of those weapons, compared with those guns' original locations on the edge of the hangar deck. *National Museum of Naval Aviation*

An aerial view along the starboard side of *Intrepid* on February 20, 1945, includes a clear view of the new sponson for a quad 40 mm gun mount on the hangar deck near the stern. Farther forward on the hangar deck, midway between the stern and the island, is the sponson and 40 mm gun mount installed at Pearl Harbor in July 1944. *National Museum of Naval Aviation*

On March 18, 1945, USS *Intrepid* was operating with Task Group 58.4 southeast of the island of Kyushu, in the Japanese home islands, when an enemy twin-engine aircraft, reportedly a Mitsubishi G4M Betty bomber, was sighted approaching the carrier. Here, antiaircraft shells directed at that airplane are bursting in the distance to the rear of the ship. Two relatively large bursts, possibly errant shots fired by nearby US warships, are very close to the carrier. Shrapnel from a 5-inch shell fired from a nearby ship injured a number of *Intrepid* crewmen.

Hits were registered on the Japanese plane, and it is in flames, on a downward trajectory just above the water. Subsequently, the aircraft crashed close to the starboard side of *Intrepid*, spraying a cloud of gasoline and hot metal into the hangar bay through the open roller doors near the forward crane.

A photographer aboard the carrier USS *Enterprise* (CV-6) snapped this photo at the moment of impact of the suicide plane offse the starboard side of USS *Intrepid*. The fireball from the crash is visible above the flight deck and through the forward bay of the hangar. The explosion caused a fire in the hangar, which firefighters quickly extinguished. Splinters from the explosion damaged the forward bay near the aircraft crane.

Smoke is boiling up from the forward starboard hangar bay after the near miss of the kamikaze aircraft on March 18, 1945.

Quick action by firefighters on USS *Intrepid* saved the carrier from significant damage. Total casualties from the kamikaze attack and the friendly-fire shell burst were one crewman killed and one officer and forty-three men wounded.

At the upper right, a single-engine plane, likely an A6M Zero, is coming in from astern in a suicide run during the April 16, 1945, attack. In the foreground is the blurry image of a folded aircraft wing on the flight deck of *Intrepid*.

Almost a month after the March 18, 1945, near miss of a kamikaze plane off Kyushu, on April 16, 1945, *Intrepid* and Task Group 58.4 were attacked by kamikazes again, in multiple attacks through the afternoon while operating off Okinawa in support of the subsequent US invasion of that island that began on April 1. Early in the action, two kamikazes were shot down close to the carrier. A photographer caught this image of a plume of water towering over the ship, from a plane that was shot down and crashed off *Intrepid*'s starboard side early in the action.

Shell bursts from 5-inch guns are peppering the sky at high and low altitudes during the April 16 kamikaze attack. Near misses of aircraft or bombs have caused geysers of water on the aft port and starboard quarters of the carrier.

A photographer on the flight deck of the carrier USS *Yorktown* (CV-10) snapped this photograph of *Intrepid* under attack evidently at the same instant as the preceding photo, as explosions erupt on the aft port and starboard quarters of the ship.

USS *Intrepid* took a direct hit from a kamikaze at 1336 on the afternoon of April 16, 1945, when an A6M Zero fighter crashed into the aft part of the flight deck. Its engine and an armor-piercing bomb shot through the flight deck. The bomb struck the armored deck of the hangar, dishing it 4 inches deep, and then ricocheted upward, exploding about 3 feet above the deck. A photographer on the island of *Intrepid* took this view of two crewmen running forward on the flight deck, with smoke pouring out of the hole in that deck.

Smoke boils out of the hole in the flight deck following the kamikaze hit on April 16. In the foreground, a tractor is parked on the deck, while 20 mm gunners (*to the right*) watch for possible targets through the smoke. Aircraft with wings folded are spotted aft of the hole in the deck.

Firefighters near the aft end of the island are combating the fires from the kamikaze attack on April 16. They were able to extinguish the fires in under one hour: proof of the proficiency they had attained after enduring several kamikaze strikes over the preceding months.

SB2C Helldiver dive-bombers are flying past on the afternoon of April 16, 1945, after the Japanese suicide-plane attack on *Intrepid*; the wounded carrier is proceeding with other ships of Task Group 58.4. The up arrow on the left wing of the SB2Cs indicate they are from USS Bennington (CV-20). Smoke continues to issue out of the aft part of the hangar. The kamikaze strike rendered the aft elevator inoperable. Late in the day, the ship was ordered to retire to the task group's refueling area, where the damage was assessed.

USS *Intrepid* exhibits a list to port on the afternoon of April 16, following the kamikaze attack. Planes are spotted on the forward and aft parts of the flight deck: by 1615 on that afternoon, *Intrepid* had recovered all of her aircraft that were airborne during the kamikaze attack and had not landed on other carriers. *National Museum of Naval Aviation*

In another photo taken late in the afternoon of April 16, 1945, *Intrepid* is proceeding under her own power, with smoke and steam still streaming from the hangar. Water sprayed into the hangar during the firefighting effort is streaming out of the forward bays of the hangar. *National Museum of Naval Aviation*

After the fires in the hangar of *Intrepid* had been extinguished on April 16, 1945, a photographer took this view of the hangar to illustrate part of the sprinkler system in the overhead. Ironically, the planes in the hangar not destroyed by the blast and fires in the hangar were rendered useless by the salt water sprayed by the sprinklers.

Crewmen are clearing casualties and wreckage from the hangar of *Intrepid* following the April 16 kamikaze attack. The men in the right foreground are carrying out a body. In the left background is a burned-out TBF/TBM Avenger. *National Museum of Naval Aviation*

The impact of the kamikaze plane on April 16 created this hole in the flight deck. *Intrepid*'s war diary described the hole as 12 by 14 feet in size. Wreckage of the wooden planks, steel deck, and aircraft-securing rails (with U-shaped cutouts, for tying down planes to the flight deck) surrounds the part of the opening depicted in this photo taken on April 16, 1945. Fire hoses are routed through the hole and down into the hangar.

The hole in the flight deck where the bomb and the engine of the kamikaze plane crashed through is viewed from below in the hangar. In the path of those missiles were longitudinal girders of a transverse bent (a tall, lateral beam), part of frame 150, which the bomb and the engine tore apart. Below the lateral bent is a destroyed Curtiss Helldiver.

A wrecked aircraft and damage to the hangar of *Intrepid* are depicted in a photo that accompanied the official report of damage incurred by the April 16, 1945, kamikaze strike.

In another view of the hangar of *Intrepid* after the kamikaze strike, the space in the foreground is flooded with water from the firefighting effort. In the background are burned-out aircraft.

Crewmen of USS *Intrepid* continue to clear out the hangar following the kamikaze attack. In the foreground is the front end of an Avenger; in the background are Helldivers.

Two crewmen scurry around the wreckage of an Avenger, side number 105, and a Corsair, side number 69, in the hangar. Frame 127 is marked faintly on the vertical girder above the Corsair's cowling ring.

Late in the afternoon of April 16, 1945, a burned-out Vought F4U-1D Corsair, side number 25, is being jettisoned from the deck-edge elevator. Forty planes in the hangar were destroyed in the kamikaze attack that day.

After the damage to *Intrepid* was inspected on April 17, the ship was ordered to steam to Ulithi for repairs. She arrived there on April 19. Here, repairs to the flight deck are underway at Ulithi on April 30. In the background are the foremast, forward smokestack, and cranes of the repair ship USS *Ajax* (AR-6), which assisted with the repairs. During this work, it was discovered that elevators #2 and #3 required repairs that could not be performed at Ulithi, so the carrier was ordered to Hunters Point via Pearl Harbor for permanent repairs.

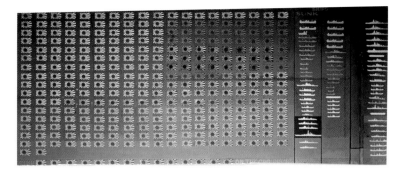

At Ulithi on May 1, 1945, a photographer recorded this image of *Intrepid*'s scoreboard: an area on the starboard side of the island where the symbols for destroyed aircraft and ships were applied. The Japanese flags represent aircraft kills, while the silhouettes of ships (*to the right*) represent various types of enemy ships sent to Davy Jones's locker. In World War II, *Intrepid*'s gun crews were credited with shooting down thirteen Japanese planes and assisting in shooting down five others. Her air groups shot down 160 aircraft and destroyed eighty-six on the ground. The aircrews also sank eleven ships, damaged forty-one, and likely sank two.

A photo from May 21, 1945, shows damage to elevator #3 from the April 16 attack. The lateral beams were warped and, at certain places, fractured, and the deck of the elevator was perforated by splinters. Frame 130 is indicated to the left.

A view facing forward inside the hangar of *Intrepid* during permanent repairs at Hunters Point on May 21, 1945, incorporates much of the previous view of the damage to the flight deck and the transverse bent at frame 150 (*top*) taken on the date of the kamikaze attack, April 16. A faint dotted line traces the path of the Japanese bomb and plane fragments from the upper left to the approximate point of the bomb's detonation, slightly to the right of center. Above the wooden scaffolding in the right background is a temporary gallery deck.

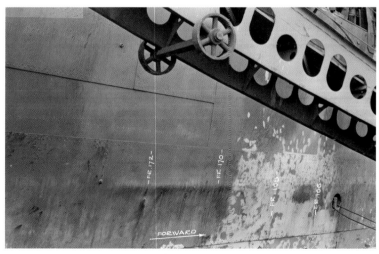

Not all the damage to *Intrepid* in the kamikaze attack of April 16, 1945, was caused by the crash of the plane on the flight deck. The explosion of a kamikaze that was "splashed" off the starboard side of the carrier caused a depression in the shell plates in the area from approximately frames 166 to 175. The photo is dated May 21, 1945.

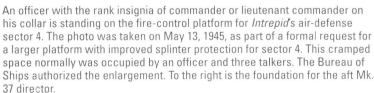

Showing space occupied by officer and three talkers. Comparativ... Shows inadequacy of space and splinter protection. This station controls all 0mm. and 20mm. in Sector 4. Sector 3 is similar.

Sector 4 M. G. Control Station

Sector 3 is similar

KEEP OUT

View from Forward

An officer with the rank insignia of commander or lieutenant commander on his collar is standing on the fire-control platform for *Intrepid*'s air-defense sector 4. The photo was taken on May 13, 1945, as part of a formal request for a larger platform with improved splinter protection for sector 4. This cramped space normally was occupied by an officer and three talkers. The Bureau of Ships authorized the enlargement. To the right is the foundation for the aft Mk. 37 director.

The area of the sector 4 fire control platform in the background of the preceding photo is seen, facing aft. The device in the foreground is a Target Designator Transmitter and Rack unit Mk. 3. Binoculars would be installed on the swiveling mount on top of the designator. The designator allowed the operator to acquire incoming enemy aircraft and transmit information on the location and path of the target to the directors.

CHAPTER 2
Cold War and the Space Age

Following the Japanese surrender, USS *Intrepid* departed from the western Pacific for the United States in October 1945. She was decommissioned on March 22, 1947, and transferred to the Pacific Reserve Fleet and placed in "mothballs," or long-term storage, at San Francisco, California. The ship is seen from the starboard side while docked at San Francisco around 1948, with much of her rigging removed and protective "igloos" placed over 40 mm gun mounts to keep the elements out. *Author's collection*

At the end of World War II, the United States had 6,768 combat ships, including ninety-nine aircraft carriers, far in excess of peacetime needs. Some ships were scrapped, others were used as targets, a few remained active, but many, including *Intrepid*, were placed in reserve. On August 15, 1946, *Intrepid* was designated "in commission in reserve" as a unit of the San Francisco Group, Pacific Reserve Fleet. On March 22, 1947, her status was changed to "out of commission in reserve." This change, commonly referred to as being placed in mothballs, meant that her machinery and equipment were coated with preservatives, her spaces were sealed and dehumidifiers were installed, and large domes containing desiccants were placed over her 40 mm batteries.

As *Intrepid* slumbered, there were many changes in naval aviation. Aircraft, which had grown increasingly heavy during World War II, continued to increase in size. Jet aircraft were introduced, 20 mm light antiaircraft armament was increasingly viewed as ineffective, and advances were made in guided missiles.

The Ships Characteristics Board (SCB), which had replaced the General Board in 1945, studied these developments with regard to aircraft carriers and also carried forward the General Board's belief that the Essex-class carriers had become increasingly unstable due to ever-growing topside weight in the form of armament, ammunition, heavier aircraft (which had increased as much as 50 percent between the time of the design and the end of the war), and radar installations.

In 1946, the SCB put forward design SCB-27, "a carrier capable [of] operating offensively with new heavy aircraft, jet aircraft, pilotless aircraft or guided missiles, as selected." In January 1947, SCB-27A was introduced, which was to entail "the minimum alterations necessary to permit Essex-class carriers to operate present or prospective fighter[-]type aircraft and the largest and heaviest attack[-]type aircraft now considered feasible without requiring major structural changes."

The first SCB-27A ship, *Oriskany*, was budgeted for fiscal year 1948, with additional ships to be modernized in subsequent years.

When war broke out in Korea in June 1950, many feared it would escalate into World War III, and the timeline of the modification program was advanced. That same year, the British began experimenting with a steam catapult aboard HMS *Perseus*. The steam catapult promised considerably more power than the previous hydropneumatic catapults used. On January 14, 1952, *Perseus* demonstrated these catapults to US officials in Philadelphia.

The steam catapult was adopted, which, along with other improvements, was incorporated in SCB-27C conversion, the standard to which *Intrepid* was modified.

To undertake this conversion, *Intrepid* was withdrawn from the reserve fleet in California on Saturday, February 9, 1952, and was partially reactivated (chiefly her propulsion and navigation spaces), and the ship was placed back in commission, in reserve.

A notable speaker that day was VAdm. T. L. Sprague, commander of the Pacific Fleet and, almost a decade earlier, *Intrepid*'s first CO. On March 12, she got underway, steaming to her birthplace, Newport News Shipbuilding and Drydock Company. She arrived seventeen days later. On April 9, 1952, she tied up at Norfolk Naval Operating Base, was again decommissioned, and entered the shipyard for modernization.

With the work complete, *Intrepid* was recommissioned in reserve at 1430 hours on June 18, 1954, in a ceremony that included Mrs. John H. Hoover, who had christened *Intrepid* in 1943. On October 15, *Intrepid* shed her reserve status and rejoined the fleet, featuring the first American-built steam catapult. The next month she conducted sea tests of the new catapult system. Reflecting changes in the US Navy designation, she was now CVA-11—reflecting her attack carrier role.

Beyond the catapults, the conversion had been extensive: strengthening the flight deck, moving the #3 elevator to the starboard deck edge, enlarging other elevators, removing belt armor and adding blisters, removing the 5-inch twin mounts and reducing and reconfiguring the remaining 5-inch battery, adding fourteen new twin 3-inch/50 antiaircraft guns, and reconstructing the island.

Rejoining the fleet, *Intrepid* operated routinely in the Atlantic and Mediterranean until late 1956.

The British had introduced another notable advance in carrier design, the angled flight deck. On September 29, 1956, *Intrepid* entered New York Naval Shipyard for further modernization, including installation of an angled flight deck, as part of program SCB-125. With the angled deck, the aircraft landing area was slanted several degrees off to port, enabling aircraft to easily "go around" in the event of recovery difficulties. The benefits this brought to carrier aviation operating safety can hardly be overemphasized. To improve seakeeping, the flight deck's forward end was blended into the upper hull form, creating the so-called "hurricane" bow. It also provided a covered location for the carriers' secondary conning station, whose portholes, visible across the upper bow plating, were a distinctive feature of the ships such as *Intrepid* receiving the SCB-125 modernization. Due to the reconfiguration of the ship, and decreased utility of the guns, *Intrepid*'s antiaircraft gun suite was reduced in the process, with nine of the fourteen 3-inch/50 mounts installed in 1954 being removed.

Seven months after entering the yard, *Intrepid* emerged in April 1957, with fitting-out being accomplished in Bayonne, New Jersey, in the last weeks of that month. She left Bayonne, work complete, on May 7. Late that year, after refresher training and operation in European waters, *Intrepid* crossed the Arctic Circle, which made the ship's company and air group members of the Royal Order of the Blue Nose.

For the remainder of the 1950s *Intrepid* operated primarily in the Atlantic, Mediterranean, Caribbean, and Baltic areas. This continued into the early 1960s as well. The ship's classification was changed again on March 31, 1962, becoming CVS-11, an antisubmarine warfare carrier, with a corresponding change in aircraft.

Only two months later, *Intrepid* entered a new age, as she was selected to recover astronaut Scott Carpenter—a Navy lieutenant commander—and his Mercury capsule *Aurora 7* upon splashdown near the Bahamas. En route to the recovery area, practice recoveries were made using dummy capsules. Delays in liftoff allowed *Intrepid* crewmen to have some R&R in St. Thomas. Carpenter splashed down off course on May 24, 230 miles from the nearest surface vessel. *Intrepid* launched two HSS-2 helicopters, then the world's fastest, to recover Carpenter, successfully returning him to the carrier. Because of the distance, however, *Aurora 7* was picked up by the closer USS *John R. Pierce*.

In June and July 1962, *Intrepid* hosted midshipman cruises, venturing north to Quebec. But for routine overhaul, *Intrepid* continued to operate normally in the Atlantic and Caribbean, participating in Navy Day celebrations in New York in 1963.

Intrepid returned to the space age in 1965, since she had again been selected as a recovery ship, this time for Gemini 3. After having taken up position on March 19, she retrieved Lt. Cmdr. John Young and Maj. Virgil Grissom and their capsule "Molly Brown" when the first manned Gemini flight splashed down 45 miles short of their intended splashdown point on March 23, 1965. *Intrepid* returned the astronauts and the spacecraft to Cape Kennedy.

On April 9, 1965, *Intrepid* entered New York Naval Shipyard for FRAM II (Fleet Rehabilitation and Modernization) overhaul, receiving the SCB-144 upgrade. This involved installing a new 63-ton bulbous bow that housed SQS-23 sonar. Work on *Intrepid* was the last FRAM job of the storied shipyard, which had been slated for closure by Defense Secretary Robert McNamara. In September, with the work 75 percent complete, *Intrepid* was moved down the East River to the Naval Supply Depot in Bayonne for completion of the $10 million project. The carrier returned to fleet service in November 1965, beginning with refresher training.

Intrepid is viewed from astern during storage at San Francisco. The enlarged sponson and the additional splinter shield for a second quadruple 40 mm gun mount on the fantail, installed at Hunters Point, San Francisco, in early 1945, are in the foreground. *Author's collection*

The forward section of *Intrepid* is in the background in this ca. 1948 photograph taken from the starboard side. The antenna masts and 20 mm gun mounts had been removed.

The enlarged sponson and splinter shields for the two 40 mm gun mounts are seen from directly astern. Between them is the structure for the directors associated with those gun mounts, installed in early 1945. There were two directors, the aft one being lower than the forward one. Another feature that dated to the January–February 1945 modernization was the 40 mm gun sponson at the hangar-deck level on the starboard side. This sponson was extended outward to give the gun mount a better field of fire. *Author's collection*

Around 1950, USS *Intrepid* is surrounded by other ships of the Pacific Reserve Fleet at Hunters Point.

In February 1952, *Intrepid* was taken out of mothballs and sailed from San Francisco to Newport News Shipbuilding and Drydock Company, Newport News, Virginia, where she had been built a decade earlier. *Intrepid* is seen during that voyage, with two Martin PBM Mariners (one of which has the wings removed), a Vought Corsair, and a wingless North American SNJ trainer secured to the flight deck. The carrier's number, 11, has been painted on the side of the smokestack. *National Museum of Naval Aviation*

In a dockside photo of *Intrepid* at Newport News on March 29, 1952, the tail of the Martin PBM is visible above the deck-edge elevator, and three aircraft that appear to be Vought Corsairs are spotted forward of the elevator. An igloo shelter is positioned over the quadruple 40 mm gun mount on the forecastle, and a small, cylindrical shelter is over the Mk. 51 director to the port of the gun mount. *Courtesy of Sargeant Memorial Collection, Norfolk Public Library*

At Newport News, from April 1952 to June 1954, *Intrepid* was essentially rebuilt in order for her to continue to serve in the jet age. *Intrepid* was redesignated as an attack carrier in October 1952 and assigned the number CVA-11. She was one of six Essex-class carriers to receive the SCB-27C modernizations, which included an array of changes, such as a reinforced flight deck to handle the increased weight of jet aircraft; elimination of the four twin 5-inch/38-caliber gun mounts and tripod foremast; installation of hull blisters and a smaller, streamlined island, a pole mast, and a taller smokestack; and new radars. The -27C program also featured an angled flight deck, C11 steam catapults, removal of the aft elevator, and installation of a new deck-edge elevator on the starboard side aft of the island. *Intrepid* would not receive the angled flight deck until a later modernization. *US Navy*

Intrepid is viewed above from the aft-port quarter during SCB-27A modernization at Newport News on May 14, 1954, showing the new starboard deck-edge elevator, covered-over aft elevator, and diminished island with built-in smokestack. The ship's quadruple 40 mm gun mounts had been replaced by twin 3-inch/50-caliber automatic gun mounts, including two on the fantail and two on the forecastle. *US Navy*

USS *Intrepid* was recommissioned on June 20, 1954, following her modernization at Newport News. As seen in a frontal elevated view of *Intrepid* off Norfolk on June 18, 1954, the flag bridge was one level below the navigating bridge, with the flag bridge jutting farther forward. The C11 steam catapults were in the two long, dark strips on the forward part of the flight deck; the catapults were angled toward starboard of the deck centerline. *US Navy*

In another photo of *Intrepid* at Norfolk on June 18, 1954, a series of 35-foot NT-66047 whip antennas are along the starboard side of the flight deck. The Mk. 37 directors, one of which is visible above the navigating bridge, had been revamped and now were equipped with Mk. 25 fire-control antennas. Both the deck-edge elevators are folded up; they were designed to do this in order to allow the ship to fit within the confines of the Panama Canal locks. *US Navy*

As seen in an aerial view at Norfolk, Virginia, on June 18, 1954, angled extensions were added to the starboard flight deck to the front and the rear of the new deck-edge elevator. Painted on the flight deck are safety lines, border and centerlines, and the ship's hull number, 11. *US Navy*

Intrepid is underway in Hampton Roads, Virginia, two days after her recommissioning, on June 18, 1954. The radar antenna atop her superstructure, forward of the pole mast, is the SPS-8 height finder. On the outriggers of the pole mast are, *left*, the SPN-6 carrier-controlled approach (CCA) antenna, and, *right*, the SPS-12 air-search antenna. Atop the pole mast is a TACAN (tactical air navigation) antenna. Visible above the front of the smokestack is a World War II–vintage SC air-search radar antenna. Various other radar and electronic-warfare antennas were on the pole mast. *Naval History and Heritage Command*

USS *Intrepid* is underway at sea in August 1954. The two twin 3-inch/50-caliber gun mounts on the forecastle that were present in the June 1954 photos had been removed as a weight-saving measure. *Intrepid* lacked a closed bow, also called the hurricane bow, that other Essex-class carriers with angled flight decks had been fitted with during modernizations; *Intrepid* would gain such a bow in the 1956–57 SCR-125 modernization, when she also would gain an angled flight deck. The new hull blisters extended up to the hangar deck, and they are most evident in the flat ledges their tops formed along that deck amidships. *National Museum of Naval Aviation*

Intrepid is operating in the Caribbean off Guantánamo Bay, Cuba, during her post-recommissioning shakedown cruise on February 9, 1955. In addition to the 3-inch gun mounts, the carrier now had eight single 5-inch/38-caliber dual-purpose gun mounts, four mounts per side. The aircraft on the flight deck appear to be McDonnell F2H Banshees. *National Museum of Naval Aviation*

Two 5-inch/38-caliber guns and, in the background, a twin 3-inch/50-caliber automatic gun mount are engaged in firing practice in October 1955. The 5-inch guns were designated as dual purpose, meaning they were effective against both air and surface targets.

Intrepid is at anchor in an unidentified harbor sometime between approximately late May 1955 and early September 1956; this time frame is based on the presence of North American AJ-2 Savage medium bombers, which were embarked on this carrier during this time frame only. Other types of aircraft are also on the flight deck, including McDonnell F2H Banshees and Douglas AD Skyraiders to the rear. *San Diego and Air Space Museum*

A Vought F7U-3M Cutlass, side number 308, is advancing to launching position on USS *Intrepid* in February 1956. The -3M version of the Cutlass twin-engine jet fighter was armed with up to four AAM-N-2 Sparrow I air-to-air missiles.

Marked on its tail for Attack Squadron 83 (VA-83), a Vought F7U-3M Cutlass, side number 308, is being prepared for a catapult launch from USS *Intrepid* in 1956. A Piasecki HUP Retriever helicopter on plane-guard duty is hovering in the background.

During modernization of *Intrepid* between September 1956 and May 1957, an enclosed escalator was installed on the starboard exterior of the hull, below the island, for pilots to move more readily from the hangar deck to the flight deck.

A Vought F7U-3M Cutlass is launching from the starboard catapult of *Intrepid* in 1956. To the lower right is the forward starboard 5-inch/38-caliber gun mount.

During a cruise in June 1956, a Beechcraft Twin Beech is warming its engines in the foreground on the flight deck of USS *Intrepid.* A variety of aircraft from Carrier Air Group 8 are on deck, including a Vought F7U Cutlass in the right foreground, to the rear of which are dark-colored Grumman S2F Trackers and Douglas AD Skyraiders. *National Museum of Naval Aviation*

A Vought F7U-3M Cutlass is being prepared for launching from *Intrepid* on June 5, 1956. The booth jutting from the island, above the center of the right wing of the Cutlass, is primary fly control, or "PriFly." Between the times the preceding photo and this one were taken, the lower front of the island and flag bridge were painted black, ostensibly to mask soot from jet exhaust of aircraft that were taking off.

From late September 1956 to May 1957, USS *Intrepid* underwent the SCB-125 modernization at the New York Navy Yard. This work including the installation of an angled, reinforced flight deck and a mirror landing system: an optical device invented by the British to assist pilots in ascertaining that they were in the correct glide approach for a safe landing. Another major change in this modernization was the rebuilding of the bow. The original open bow was removed, as depicted in this photo, and a closed, or hurricane, bow was installed. *Collection of the* Intrepid *Sea, Air & Space Museum; gift of the family of Robert Salmanowitz Sr., P2016.43.149*

USS *Intrepid* is at anchor off the Navy base, New York Navy Yard, in this series of six photos taken on May 6, 1957, at or near the end of her SCB-125 modernization. The carrier now sports a closed bow, also called a hurricane bow, in the center of which are portholes for the new secondary conning station inside the structure. The angled flight deck also has been installed. At the front of the angled flight deck is the relocated port deck-edge elevator, with a curved front edge. *US Navy*

Intrepid is observed from the port side off New York Navy Yard on May 6, 1957. The hull number, 11, is painted in white with black shadowing on the side of the island. The fantail remained of open design, with 3-inch gun mounts still located in tubs below the rear of the flight deck. *US Navy*

A major SCB-125 modification not visible in these photos was the lengthened forward elevator. An admiral's barge is visible on the flight deck, adjacent to the top of the aircraft crane. *US Navy*

The aircraft crane just forward of the starboard deck-edge elevator was a recent addition. As part of the SCB-125 modernization, the old primary fly station, or PriFly, on the port side of the island had been removed, and a greatly expanded PriFly had been built farther back and higher up on the island; the main part was on the port side, with a rear extension wrapping around the rear of the island. The rear extension is visible here, immediately to port of the aft Mk. 37 director.

A frontal photo of *Intrepid* offers a view of the new enclosed bow. The secondary conning station, which was an emergency steering and navigation compartment, was in the upper center of the closed bow. Seven portholes for that station are visible, with their steel covers lowered. Two overruns for the catapults are on the enclosed bow.

Boats are moored to boat booms extended from the hull of *Intrepid* in this photo taken from astern on the same occasion as the two preceding photos. A dish antenna for a fire-control radar is above the twin 3-inch guns on the starboard side of the fantail. The new PriFly is clearly visible, jutting from the port side of the island. Similar to the navigating bridge, PriFly had windows that tilted outward at the tops.

USS *Intrepid*, *left of center*, and USS *Valley Forge* (CVS-45), to *Intrepid's* right, are moored to the same pier at Naval Station Norfolk, Virginia, around 1957. Although both carriers were from the Essex class, *Intrepid* presented a much more modern appearance, with her angled flight deck and lack of twin 5-inch gun mounts to the front and rear of the island. *Valley Forge* never was subjected to the SCB-27 or SCB-125 modernizations, retaining her straight flight deck, open bow, and twin 5-inch gun mounts throughout her postwar career.

While a Douglas AD-6 Skyraider, Bureau Number (BuNo) 139678 and modex 411, assigned to VA-25 ("Fist of the Fleet"), was landing on USS *Intrepid* on May 30, 1959, a drop tank with fuel in it came loose and ignited. Here, the tank has skidded forward on the flight deck, and the plane is engulfed in smoke and fuel vapor.

Fleet oiler USS *Neosho* (AO-143), *center*, is refueling USS *Intrepid* and destroyer USS *Cone* (DD-866) during Exercise Lantflex 2-58, in the Caribbean, on November 12, 1958. Refueling at sea allowed warships to remain on or near station. The oiler would maintain a steady course, at speed, while the ships being refueled maintained as constant an interval as possible, around 100 feet, from the oiler. *Randy Fagan, Floating Drydock.com*

Deck crewmen are racing to assist in extinguishing the flames as fire roars below and to the rear of AD-6 BuNo 139678. *National Museum of Naval Aviation*

One type of fighter deployed on *Intrepid* in the late 1950s was the McDonnell F3H-2N Demon. According to the original caption of this photo, this F3H-2N is bolting the flight deck, which means it failed to catch an arrestor cable and has accelerated to take off for another attempt to land. However, the arrestor hook is not extended in this photo, so it seems more likely the pilot was performing touch-and-go landings.

USS *Intrepid* (*foreground*) and USS *Independence* (CVA-62), a Forrestal-class aircraft carrier, are docked next to each other at their home port, Norfolk, Virginia, around spring 1961. Before the supercarrier *Independence* was commissioned in 1960, *Intrepid* claimed the nickname "Mighty I," but after *Independence* became operational, *Intrepid* yielded her original nickname to the larger carrier and adopted the new nickname "Fighting I." *National Museum of Naval Aviation*

Planes of Carrier Air Group 6 are on the flight deck of *Intrepid* during a US Sixth Fleet cruise in the Mediterranean on August 28, 1961. The "AF" tail codes of CVG-6 are visible on the aircraft, which include A4D Skyhawks of VA-66 and VA-76, F4D Skyrays of VF-162, AD-6 Skyraiders of VA-65, and F8U Crusaders from VF-33. *National Museum of Naval Aviation*

In another view of *Intrepid* cruising in the Mediterranean on August 28, 1961, the same Skyrays in the foreground of the preceding photo are spotted on the port side of the forward part of the flight deck, while the Skyraider to the front of the island is no longer present. On the port side of the hull, a Crusader with wings folded is on the deck-edge elevator. *National Museum of Naval Aviation*

USS *Intrepid* is at anchor in the harbor of Genoa, Italy, on October 21, 1961. All the aircraft spotted on the flight deck forward of the island are F8U Crusaders. A mix of aircraft types are farther aft, with AD-6 Skyraiders occupying the rear of the flight deck. *National Museum of Naval Aviation*

The fourth manned Mercury space capsule, nicknamed *Aurora 7* and manned by astronaut Scott Carpenter, splashed down northeast of Puerto Rico, following three orbits of the earth, on May 24, 1962. Carpenter was 250 miles from the prearranged splashdown site; however, after a forty-minute search for the capsule, a helicopter from USS *Intrepid* rescued Carpenter and brought him aboard the carrier. The capsule and several rafts dropped from a transport plane are in view.

Escorted by a Navy officer, Scott Carpenter strides across the deck of *Intrepid* following his recovery on May 24, 1962. A photographer and a cameraman in the left background are documenting the occasion.

After settling into *Intrepid* following his post-splashdown recovery, Scott Carpenter takes a congratulatory call from President John F. Kennedy.

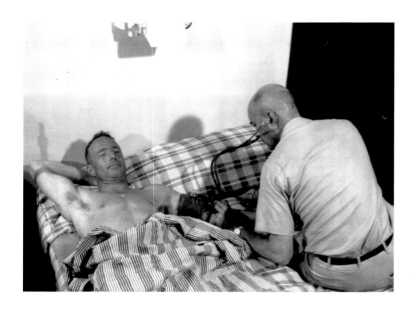

A US Navy physician is examining astronaut Scott Carpenter on USS *Intrepid* for any signs of physical problems following his splashdown in *Aurora 7*.

The Vought F8U Crusader single-engine, supersonic jet fighter was introduced to *Intrepid* by 1957; it was redesignated F-8 in 1962. The Crusader had a variable-incidence wing, seen in this prelaunching photo in the raised position. The plane, and F8U-1P, was from Light Photographic Squadron 62 (VFP-62), which was assigned to *Intrepid* from 1957 to 1962. *US Navy*

A photo of *Intrepid* at sea on March 31, 1963, provides useful details of the antenna arrays at that time. On a short pole mast on the starboard side of the top of the superstructure is an AN/SPS-29 antenna. On the port side of the top of the superstructure is an AN/SPS-30 pencil-beam height-finder antenna, immediately above which is an AN/SPN-6 carrier-controlled approach antenna. At the top of the pole mast are electronic-countermeasures antennas and, *at the center*, a TACAN antenna. *National Museum of Naval Aviation*

In the Atlantic off the US East Coast on April 21, 1963, a C-1 Trader has just launched from the starboard catapult. Aft of the island, to the starboard side of the flight deck, is a tilted antenna mast, with eight whip antennas on top of it. *National Museum of Naval Aviation*

USS *Intrepid* is viewed from the starboard side with her air group embarked during a Mediterranean cruise around 1964. Douglas Skyraiders (redesignated from AD to A-1 in 1962) and Grumman Trackers (redesignated from S2F to S-2 in 1962) are spotted on the forward part of the flight deck. What appear to be Kaman Seasprites and a pair of Sikorsky Sea King helicopters are aft of the island. *National Museum of Naval Aviation*

On July 23, 1964, crewmen in dress whites are lining the rails of USS *Intrepid* as the carrier docks at Naval Station Rota, Spain. Much of the deck markings are visible, including the outline around the forward elevator. *National Museum of Naval Aviation*

A banner that reads "INTREPID HAS A DATE WITH 'GUS' AND 'JOHN'" is rigged along the flight deck below the bridges. This was in reference to the carrier's role on March 23, 1965, in recovering the astronaut crew of the Gemini 3 space capsule, nicknamed "Molly Brown": Virgil "Gus" Grissom and John Young. *US Navy*

A Navy diver is suspended on a line from a Sikorsky SH-3 Sea King, BuNo 148979 and side number 53, from Helicopter Antisubmarine Squadron 3 (HS-3), assigned to *Intrepid*, during the recovery of astronauts Grissom and Young on March 23, 1965.

After splashdown of "Molly Brown" in the Atlantic, northeast of the Turks and Caicos Islands, a Sikorsky Sea King from USS *Intrepid* is hovering near the capsule. Green dye had been released in the sea to assist recovery crews in locating the capsule.

USS *Intrepid* has come alongside the "Molly Brown" Gemini 3 capsule during the recovery operation following the successful Gemini-Titan 3 flight on March 23, 1965. Three Navy divers are standing on the flotation collar around the capsule. They will secure a hoist cable to the capsule.

An aircraft crane on *Intrepid* has just lifted the Gemini capsule from the ocean. Hovering in the background is a Sikorsky SH-3 helicopter. *Naval History and Heritage Command*

The Gemini capsule is viewed from another perspective as it is hoisted toward the deck-edge elevator. The yellow flotation collar is still attached to the capsule.

Civilian personnel, apparently from NASA, are guiding the "Molly Brown" capsule onto a cart on the deck-edge elevator on March 23, 1965. The capsule survives in the collections of the National Air and Space Museum.

Shortly after *Intrepid* and crew completed the recovery of the Gemini 3 astronauts and capsule, the carrier steamed from Norfolk to the New York Navy Yard for a six-month modernization. There, *Intrepid* underwent a FRAM II (Fleet Rehabilitation and Modernization II) refitting, the last one performed by the New York Navy Yard before it closed.

The forward part of the flight deck of USS *Intrepid* is viewed from above during her time in drydock at New York in 1965. Late that summer, the ship was moved to Bayonne, New Jersey, where FRAM II work was completed in October 1965.

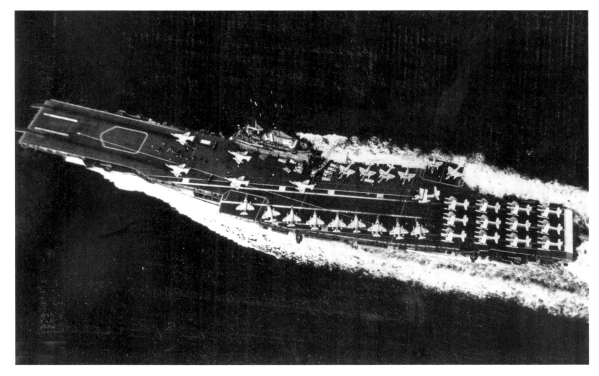

Aircraft of Carrier Antisubmarine Air Group 10 (CVSG-10) are embarked on USS *Intrepid* at sea on December 16, 1965. Most of the aircraft on the flight deck are Douglas A-4 Skyhawks. To the rear are a dozen Douglas A-1 Skyraiders. A Grumman Tracker is inboard of the starboard deck-edge elevator.

CHAPTER 3
Vietnam

One of the roles of USN aircraft carriers was to refuel and resupply smaller ships at sea. here, USS *Intrepid* is refueling the destroyer USS *Borie* (DD-704) on February 20, 1966. Two months later, *Intrepid* would commence her first of three combat tours of Vietnam, with Carrier Air Wing 10 embarked each time. For these tours, undertaken in support of the Seventh Fleet, *Intrepid* was repurposed from an antisubmarine carrier to an attack carrier. *Randy Fagan, Floating Drydock.com*

When the FRAM II overhaul was completed in November 1965, *Intrepid* was one of the most up-to-date antisubmarine warfare carriers in the US fleet. That, however, had nothing to do with her next major assignment.

On February 26, 1966, Secretary of Defense Robert McNamara announced during defense appropriation hearings that *Intrepid* would be deployed to Vietnam, stating, "In order to maintain the attack carrier force off Vietnam, we are, as I noted, temporarily deploying one of the Atlantic-based carriers, *Intrepid*, to Southeast Asia. Very minor modifications are required on this vessel to permit it to operate light attack aircraft, and it can be quickly reassigned to its anti-submarine role. What is involved mainly is a change in the aircraft complement. The anti-submarine air group is being retained in the active fleet, thus giving us the capability to operate the carrier as a CVS on short notice."

The ship underwent minor modifications and embarked carrying attack aircraft. By the spring of 1966, *Intrepid* was on its way to Southeast Asia, transiting the Suez Canal on April 22. After a brief stay at Subic Bay, *Intrepid*, operating as a "special attack carrier," took her position at Dixie Station off South Vietnam.

From there, she launched her first strikes against the Viet Cong on May 15. Operating in this area for fifty-nine days, her Air Wing 10 flew almost 5,000 sorties against enemy targets. She then moved to Yankee Station in the Gulf of Tonkin, from which Air Wing 10 flew a further 2,595 sorties over a period of forty-one days. During one of these, on October 9, 1966, one of *Intrepid*'s VA-176 prop-driven A-1H Skyraiders, flown by Lt. (j.g.) Tom Patton, downed a Soviet-built MiG-17 jet while the former was on a rescue CAP mission.

Intrepid returned to the United States on November 21 for overhaul and leave. Overhaul complete, she left Norfolk on April 6 for operational readiness inspection, then on May 11, 1967, steamed again for Vietnam, along the way becoming the final US warship to go through the Suez Canal before the Six-Day War. *Intrepid* arrived at Yankee Station off North Vietnam on June 21, 1967. She remained there for 104 days, her Air Wing 10 flying over 9,000 missions, before leaving on November 25, arriving first in Subic Bay on November 30 and then at Norfolk on December 30, 1967. *Intrepid* entered Norfolk Navy Yard on January 4, 1968, for annual overhaul.

Intrepid steamed for Vietnam on June 4, 1968, arriving at Yankee Station for her third deployment at 2300 on July 23, 1968. After operating in this area for thirty days, she retired to Sasebo, Japan, for routine maintenance and R&R for the crew. On November 5 she was back on Yankee Station, striking targets in North Vietnam. With breaks for R&R in Hong Kong and Subic Bay, *Intrepid* fought from the Gulf of Tonkin until the bombing halt on North Vietnam went into effect on November 1. Then she moved south, to Dixie Station, her final posting in Vietnamese waters, where she launched attacks on southern targets until November 24, then heading for home by way of Australia and New Zealand and around Cape Horn, arriving at Norfolk Naval Station on February 8, 1969.

Later that month, she entered Philadelphia Naval Shipyard's Dry Dock #5 for overhaul, which took five months. Overhaul complete, *Intrepid* would return to her role as an antisubmarine carrier in the Atlantic Fleet, with a home port of Quonset Point, Rhode Island. On the morning of September 9, 1969, she steamed into Narragansett Bay under the command of Horus "Whitey" Moore, who had taken command on August 1, and under the guidance of a harbor pilot, *Intrepid* ran aground in full view of the assembled mass of press, dignitaries, and families awaiting arrival of the new flagship of Carrier Division 16.

Early 1970 was spent in antisubmarine warfare training in the Gulf of Mexico. From May 26 until August 22 she was in Boston Naval Shipyard for overhaul. On September 22 she steamed to Halifax, Nova Scotia, for a joint US-Canada exercise. After this exercise, she encountered a storm, causing damage that necessitated a return to Boston Naval Shipyard for repair. After repair, she returned to Quonset Point and remained in port.

On February 22, 1971, *Intrepid* left Quonset Point for the Bermuda operating area. There she conducted a sinking exercise against the former USS *Reuben James* (DE-153) on March 1. Steaming toward Quonset Point on March 4, *Intrepid* encountered heavy seas and high winds, at one point rolling a dangerous 28 degrees starboard, which caused considerable damage.

Intrepid left Quonset Point on April 16, 1971, for a six-month deployment as the flagship of Task Group 83.2, anchoring at Lisbon, Portugal, on April 28, leaving Lisbon on May 2 for participation in the NATO exercise Rusty Razor before putting into Plymouth, England, on May 10. From there she steamed to Kiel, West Germany, and entered the Baltic Sea on May 16, becoming the first carrier to conduct flight operations in the eastern Baltic, only 20 miles off the Soviet coast. She left the Baltic ten days later, bound for the Mediterranean. She arrived in Naples, Italy, on June 4, staying for one week before taking part in Operation Constellation, after which she put into Cannes, France, on June 19. Five days later she stood out from Cannes, bound for Barcelona, arriving on June 30. Leaving Barcelona on July 6, her next port of call was Hamburg, Germany, where she arrived on July 12. After one week, she then steamed toward Copenhagen, arriving on July 21. Following one week in Copenhagen, she steamed for Greenock, Scotland, arriving on August 2. Steaming from Greenock on August 11, *Intrepid* took part in NATO exercise Alert Lancer in the Norwegian Sea, making several transits across the Arctic Circle during the operation. Numerous Soviet submarines were detected during the operations, which ended on September 7. Additional Norwegian Sea exercises were conducted as Operation Agile Warrior, at the conclusion of which *Intrepid* anchored at Bergen, Norway, on September 22. Leaving on September 25 to participate in NATO operation Royal Knight, *Intrepid* found herself back at Greenock at the conclusion of the exercise on October 5. Two days later she stood out, bound for her home port, arriving at Quonset Point on October 15. On November 29, she left her home port bound for Boston Naval Shipyard for restricted availability, which would extend until January 27, 1972.

In March 1972, *Intrepid* operated in the eastern Atlantic, returning to Quonset Point on April 23. In May she passed her nuclear technical proficiency inspection, and in June her crew was certified to handle nuclear weapons. Steaming for Europe on July 11, she arrived in Copenhagen fourteen days later and then steamed into the Norwegian Sea, crossing the Arctic Circle, steaming farther east than any prior US carrier. *Intrepid*'s command history notes, "Needless to say, Soviet interest in the ship's activities was extremely high."

Returning to Quonset Point on October 20, the ship's air wing was reconfigured, reflecting a strike role, even though the ship retained its CVS antisubmarine carrier designation and capabilities. A-4E Skyhawks were brought aboard.

Intrepid steamed for the Mediterranean on November 24, 1972, on what would be her final overseas deployment. Orders were issued on March 1 that *Intrepid* would be returned to mothballs; with the ceasefire in Vietnam, Navy strength could be redistributed, and *Intrepid*, the oldest carrier, would go into retirement. On April 25, 1973, she left Rota, Spain, her final port of call in the Mediterranean, steaming toward Quonset Point. Just after 0900 on May 4, 1973, *Intrepid* steamed into Narragansett Bay under her own power for the last time. Two days later, work was begun to return *Intrepid* to the reserve fleet, and this work, rather than being done in a shipyard, as is customary, was to be done at Quonset Point by her crew, which was being reduced to half strength. Her status was changed to "in commission, in reserve" on July 23, 1973, and on March 15, 1974, she was decommissioned.

A Douglas A-4B, BuNo 145001 and modex 315, from Attack Squadron 15 (VA-15), is poised for a catapult launch from USS *Intrepid* during 1966. General-purpose high-explosive bombs with Snakeye retarding fins are shackled to the pylons. The Snakeye devices snapped open after the bombs were released, thus slowing down their descent. *National Museum of Naval Aviation*

This Douglas A-1H Skyraider, BuNo 135326, is being readied for an airstrike on Vietcong forces on May 20, 1966. On the wing pylons are napalm canisters. These aircraft were assigned to Attack Squadron 176 ("Thunderbolts"), and the squadron markings they applied to the tails of their planes were among the most colorful and striking found on Skyraiders. The closer plane is marked "LT C. A. KNOCHEL" on the cowling. *National Museum of Naval Aviation*

Douglas Skyraiders assigned to Attack Squadron 176 and Douglas Skyhawks from Attack Squadron 95 are spotted on the aft section of the flight deck of USS *Intrepid* on February 18, 1966. The nickname of VA-95 was the "Green Lizards," and stylized, elongated green lizards are emblazoned on the fuselages of these Skyhawks. The Skyraiders have not yet acquired the thunderbolt-and-bee tail art they would sport later in 1966. *National Museum of Naval Aviation*

A Douglas A-1H Skyraider from USS *Intrepid* has just landed on USS *Kearsarge* (CVS-33) to be reloaded with ammunition during airstrikes against North Vietnam during *Intrepid*'s second deployment to Vietnam, on November 7, 1967. This Skyraider was BuNo 134570 and was assigned to Attack Squadron 145 "Swordsmen," which was assigned to Carrier Air Wing 10 from May to December 1967. *National Museum of Naval Aviation*

USS *Intrepid* is underway in the South China Sea in early September 1966. Skyraiders and Skyhawks are spotted on the forward end of the flight deck. During the seven-month deployment to Vietnam that year, *Intrepid*'s Carrier Air Wing 10 flew approximately 5,000 combat missions. *National Museum of Naval Aviation*

While steaming on Yankee Station in the Gulf of Tonkin around October 1966, *Intrepid* (*in background*), was photographed from the Midway-class USS *Franklin D. Roosevelt* (CVA-42). While *Intrepid*'s air wing was populated largely by Skyhawks and Skyraiders, a variety of aircraft are on *Roosevelt*'s flight deck, from a Skyhawk and a Grumman Tracer (*in the foreground*) to Crusaders, Phantom IIs, and Douglas A-3 Skywarriors. *US Navy*

Tugboats are coming into position on the port beam of USS *Intrepid*, *left*, in preparation for the carrier's departure from Naval Station Norfolk, Virginia, for her third deployment to Vietnam, on June 4, 1968. Prominent to the rear of the island is the radome for the AN/SPN-35 aircraft control approach central radar set, a precision approach-and-landing system. On the opposite side of the pier is USS *Forrestal* (CVA-59). *National Museum of Naval Aviation*

The oiler USS *Severn* (AO-61), *center*, is simultaneously refueling USS *Intrepid*, *right*, and guided missile frigate USS *Belknap* (DLG-26), *left*, in the Atlantic on June 9, 1968. Carrier Air Wing 10 was embarked on what would be that organization's final cruise on USS *Intrepid*. *National Museum of Naval Aviation*

USS *Intrepid* arrived on Yankee Station off the coast of Vietnam on her third deployment to that theater on July 24, 1968. The carrier is seen from the starboard side during September 1968. During that month, *Intrepid*'s air group conducted intensive bombing missions against enemy targets, destroying everything from trucks and watercraft to bridges and other hard targets. *National Museum of Naval Aviation*

During operations in the Gulf of Tonkin on October 25, 1968, USS *Intrepid* (*right*), and destroyer USS *Walker* (DD-517) (*left*) are taking on fuel from fast combat-support ship USS *Camden* (AOE-2). Seven days later, on November 1, *Intrepid*'s air group ceased airstrikes on targets in North Vietnam, in accordance with a bombing halt, concentrating its efforts instead on enemy targets in South Vietnam and Laos. *US Navy*

November 15, 1968. Elevator #1 is lowered, and aircraft (Skyhawks, Crusaders, and a lone Skyraider) are tightly spotted on the aft end of the flight deck. Two dark-colored Kaman SH-2 Seasprite helicopters are near the forward end of the superstructure. *National Museum of Naval Aviation*

USS *Intrepid* is steaming through placid waters off Guantánamo Bay, Cuba, on October 30, 1969. Visible aircraft consist of Grumman Trackers, all of which have 70-million-candlepower searchlights in pods on the right wings. Farther aft are two Sikorsky SH-3 Sea King helicopters. During the modernization work in 1966, a bow anchor had been installed, and the port anchor had been eliminated and its hawsepipe covered over. *National Museum of Naval Aviation*

During a period of repairs and maintenance around January 1970, a photographer recorded this image of the bow of *Intrepid* from the floor of the drydock. On the forefoot (the bulbous bottom of the bow) is the SQS-23 sonar. Midway up the bow are the two anchors, while toward the top is the hurricane bow, with the portholes of the secondary conning station in view. *Naval History and Heritage Command*

A crewman from USS *Intrepid* is looking down on his carrier, docked at New Orleans, from the Top of the Mart, the bar on the top of the International Trade Mart, on February 5, 1970. During that year, *Intrepid* returned to her primary role, of antisubmarine warfare, operating in the Atlantic and the Mediterranean. *National Museum of Naval Aviation*

USS *Intrepid* is at sea during an operational-readiness inspection on February 24, 1971. Spotted on the forward part of the flight deck are a number of Grumman S-2 Trackers along with two Grumman E-1 Tracer airborne early-warning planes, identifiable by the large radome poised above the plane. *National Museum of Naval Aviation*

This S-2G Tracker with BuNo 153582, from Antisubmarine Squadron 24 (VS-24), "Duty Cats," Carrier Air Antisubmarine Squadron 56 (CVSG-56), is spotted on the flight deck of USS *Intrepid* on September 6, 1972. The squadron insignia is aft of the side window of the cockpit. A cover marked "VS-24" is fitted over the wing fold. The tail code of CVSG-56, "AU," is on the vertical fin and rudder. *National Museum of Naval Aviation*

Steam is rising from the starboard forward catapult track of *Intrepid* as an S-2E Tracker, modex 117, is being readied for launching during carrier-qualification trials off Quonset Point, Rhode Island, on January 11, 1971. The pylons could hold bombs, rockets, mines, and other stores. The Tracker also had a bay in the fuselage for torpedoes. *National Museum of Naval Aviation*

In the last several years of her active service, *Intrepid*'s home port was Quonset Point, Rhode Island. After *Intrepid*'s last deployment, to the Mediterranean, preparations were made to deactivate her in September 1973. She became the first US carrier to undergo the ship's-force phase of deactivation at her home port: a phase usually performed at a shipyard. This work included a wide array of tasks, from temporarily sealing the flight deck and sand-blasting exterior metal surfaces to remove paint and rust, to removing equipment from the carrier for redistribution to active-service ships. Following this work the ship was decommissioned at Quonset Point on March 15, 1974. She is seen here being towed from Quonset Point to Philadelphia for long-term storage in March 1974.

CHAPTER 4
Museum

On March 19, 1974, fleet tug USS *Shakori* (ATF-162) towed the lifeless *Intrepid* to Philadelphia to be placed in the reserve fleet. However, once she arrived in Philadelphia, the storied carrier was given a respite. On October 13, 1974, she was selected by the Navy's Bicentennial Command as the museum ship to showcase the Navy's role through the first two hundred years of our nation's history. Her hangar deck was filled with aircraft, ship models, uniforms, and other artifacts of Navy and Marine heritage. She opened in this new role at Philadelphia Naval Shipyard on July 4, 1975, her deck and hangar open to the public from Friday through Sunday. By the time the exhibit closed in September 1976, over 400,000 guests had come aboard to enjoy the celebration of Navy and Marine Corps history.

Even before thousands of visitors swarmed *Intrepid* in Philadelphia, in 1974 a group was formed in New York with a similar goal. Called Odysseys in Flight, the group, led by Michael D. Piccola, was intent on acquiring an aircraft carrier for conversion to a museum ship in the New York City area. After first considering the aircraft carrier *Lexington* (CV-16), the group soon zeroed in on *Intrepid*. In November 1978, New York real estate developer Zachary Fisher became involved with the group, and in February 1979 the *Intrepid* Museum Foundation was formed, with Fisher as executive vice president and chairman. *Intrepid* would be the first of many patriotic efforts that Zachary and his brother Larry would become involved with, including the Zachary and Elizabeth M. Fisher Armed Services Foundation, which initially provided aid and support to victims of the Beirut Marine barracks bombing, and scores more military families since, as well as the Fisher House Foundation, through which the Fishers personally dedicated more than $20 million to the construction of comfort homes for families of hospitalized military personnel. More than eighty-eight Fisher Houses now operate, which have provided eight million days of temporary lodging for 350,000 families of military personnel undergoing treatment.

USS *Intrepid* was stricken from the Naval Vessel Register in February 1982 and transferred to the *Intrepid* Museum Foundation. However, time had not been kind to *Intrepid*, and shipyard work was required for appearance and conservation and, significantly, for the daunting task of converting her from a warship, occupied by men trained to safely navigate her spaces and tolerate discomfort, to a museum that was comfortable and safe for less disciplined civilians to explore.

Intrepid left Philadelphia under tow to the Bethlehem Steel Shipyard in Hoboken, New Jersey, in February, with the lofty goal of having the repair and refit work done in time to open on July 4 of that year. The scope and cost of the repairs exceeded the original estimates, but once the work at Bethlehem was completed on June 13, 1982, *Intrepid* was towed up the Hudson and moored at her new home at Pier 86. Soon after, the workers who were to be completing the exhibit spaces went on strike.

Finally, on August 4, 1982, the *Intrepid* Museum opened. Misfortune continued, and an unusually hot and wet summer, together with the late opening, were blamed for a first-year attendance of 708,000, just over half the projected 1.4 million guests, and the resulting deficit of $3.5 million.

Visitors and revenues continued to fall short of projections, leading the *Intrepid* Museum Foundation to file Chapter 11 (reorganization) bankruptcy on July 25, 1985, citing debts of $28.4 million.

Low attendance was not the only reason for the museum's financial woes. A *New York Times* story from April 4, 1987, reported the following:

Labor racketeering by a Manhattan gang called the "Westies" siphoned off extensive funds from the air-sea-space museum on the aircraft carrier *Intrepid*, investigators disclosed yesterday.

The racketeering, Federal and New York City investigators said, principally involved the theft of box-office receipts by members of Local 1909 of the International Longshoremen's Association who were employed as ticket-sellers and through "no-show" jobs at the museum for members of the local.

According to investigators, most of the money that was stolen or obtained by fraud through fake jobs was passed along to leaders of the Westies.

Five ticket-sellers, all of whom were members of Local 1909, were dismissed on March 13, Mr. Schmidt [*Intrepid* Museum executive director Wayne Schmidt] said. The museum employs thirty-nine members of the local, he noted, as ticket sellers and in maintenance and engineering jobs.

Under a labor contract, the museum has no voice in the hiring of ticket-sellers and others in Local 1909 job jurisdictions.

Immediately after the terror attacks of September 11, 2001, the FBI requested, and was granted, the use of *Intrepid* as a command center, with helicopters again being used from her flight deck and five hundred agents making use of the ship as a several-thousand-ton bunker.

Five years later, long after her post-terror-attack reopening, *Intrepid* was in need of upkeep. While in active service, *Intrepid* was drydocked at least annually for inspection, repair, and maintenance, but by 2006 it had been decades since she had been settled on blocks in a drydock. That trip, initially delayed due to the buildup of years of silt, miring her in mud, was finally made in late 2006, when she was towed to Bayonne.

Intrepid returned to her pier in October 2008 and had a gala reopening on November 11, 2008.

After *Intrepid* was decommissioned at the Carrier Pier at Naval Air Station Quonset Point, Rhode Island, on March 15, 1974, the carrier was towed to Philadelphia for long-term storage. On February 25, 1976, the carrier entered Dry Dock #5 at Philadelphia Naval Shipyard for maintenance and repairs in preparation for the US bicentennial celebrations that summer. During that period, the carrier's hangar deck would be converted to an exhibition space commemorating the US Navy's role in American history. *National Museum of Naval Aviation*

Intrepid was opened to the public at Philadelphia on July 4, 1975, as part of the bicentennial celebrations of the US Navy and Marine Corps. Exhibits of aircraft, Navy and Marine uniforms, equipment, and memorabilia were on the flight deck and the hangar. The exhibit remained open until September 1976.

Pending *Intrepid*'s ultimate fate, a movement began to save her from scrapping and preserve her as a museum ship. In 1978, New York businessman and philanthropist Zachary Fisher and his wife, Elizabeth, founded the *Intrepid* Museum Foundation, putting up $25 million to preserve and restore the carrier at the *Intrepid* Sea, Air & Space Museum at Pier 86, Manhattan. This conceptual scale model shows *Intrepid* in the role of museum ship, with combat aircraft displayed on the flight deck. Adjacent to the carrier are planned facilities on Pier 86, on the west side of Manhattan. *National Museum of Naval Aviation*

Intrepid Museum Foundation *presents:*

THE WORLD'S ONLY **INTERNATIONAL AEROSPACE and NAVAL MEMORIAL MUSEUM**

on board the aircraft carrier U.S.S. INTREPID, CVS-11
(PROPOSED)

This diagram prepared by the *Intrepid* Museum Foundation depicts the proposed arrangement of the ship by the time of her opening to the public. Specimen Navy aircraft would be exhibited on the flight deck and in the hangar. At the rear of the hangar was an aircraft restoration area, and a theater was forward of the hangar. In spaces below the hangar were displays covering combat in World War II and *Intrepid*'s roles in recovering NASA space capsules and crews and in the US bicentennial. *National Museum of Naval Aviation*

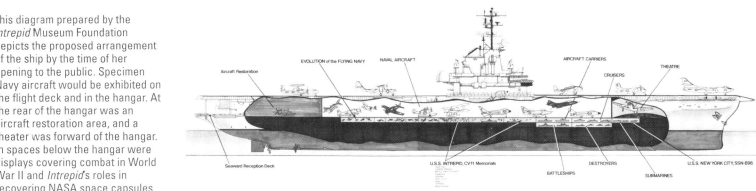

Aircraft Restoration · EVOLUTION of the FLYING NAVY · NAVAL AIRCRAFT · AIRCRAFT CARRIERS · CRUISERS · THEATRE · Seaward Reception Deck · U.S.S. INTREPID, CV-11 Memorials · BATTLESHIPS · DESTROYERS · SUBMARINES · U.S.S. NEW YORK CITY, SSN-696

PREMINARY STAGE
OPENING DAY

Intrepid Museum Foundation presents: THE WORLD'S ONLY **INTERNATIONAL AEROSPACE and NAVAL MEMORIAL MUSEUM**

on board the aircraft carrier U.S.S. INTREPID, CVS-11
(PROPOSED)

Another diagram prepared by the *Intrepid* Museum Foundation shows the displays on and in the carrier after completion of a proposed building and conversion program. Extensive displays of vintage and modern aircraft and spacecraft are on the flight deck and in the hangar, while many compartments below the hangar serve as thematic display spaces. *National Museum of Naval Aviation*

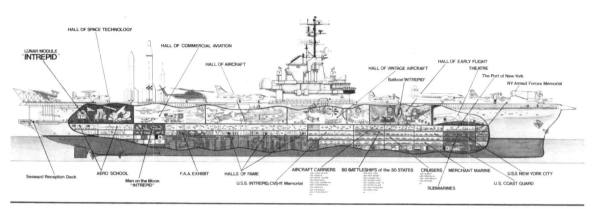

FINAL STAGE
AFTER COMPLETION OF BUILDING and CONVERSION PROGRAM

The president of the board of trustees of the *Intrepid* Museum Foundation, Zachary Fisher, stands to the right as Secretary of the Navy John F. Lehman Jr. signs a document during the official transfer of ownership of the carrier to the foundation at the Pentagon on April 27, 1981. Standing to the left is James Ean, president of the board of trustees of the *Intrepid* Museum Foundation.

On February 26, 1982, tugboats are towing *Intrepid* into New York Harbor, near the end of her transit from Philadelphia; the Verrazzano-Narrows Bridge is in the background. The ship would stop at Bayonne, New Jersey, for refitting before proceeding to her new home at Pier 86 in Manhattan.

Intrepid is viewed from the starboard quarter in New York Harbor, showing details of the raised deck-edge elevator and the stowed pole mast. A cover is installed over the top of the smokestack.

In a closer view of *Intrepid* under tow in New York Harbor on February 26, 1982, several aircraft, including a Grumman Tracker and a Grumman Trader, are secured to the forward part of the flight deck. The pole mast had been removed from the top of the island for this trip and was secured in an upright position aft of the island.

A tugboat is assisting *Intrepid*, as seen from the port quarter, in New York Harbor on February 26, 1982. In the foreground are the aft-port sponson and the fantail, including the sponson for the long-since-removed antiaircraft gun mounts.

The Grumman Tracker (*left*) and Tracer (*right*) stored on the flight deck are in sight in this frontal photo. Jutting from the port side of the top of the island is the support for the SPS-30 height-finder radar antenna.

Intrepid is seen from off its starboard stern while docked at Bayonne, New Jersey, on or around February 26, 1982. Shortly thereafter, the Bethlehem Steel plant at Bayonne began the process of converting the carrier to a museum ship, including completely repainting her.

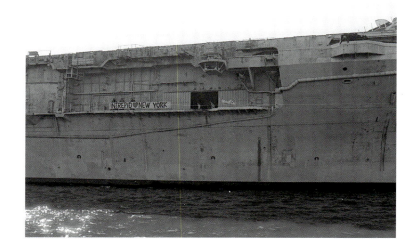

In honor of her new home, a banner reading "INTREPID [heart] NEW YORK" is rigged on the rails along the forward starboard bay of the hangar. On the round platform above the open door is a Mk. 56 Gun Fire Control System (GFCS) director. The Mk. 56 GFCS controlled the ship's twin 3-inch/50-caliber rapid-fire gun mounts.

The starboard side of *Intrepid*'s island is viewed around the time of the carrier's arrival at Bayonne, New Jersey. To the left is the radome for the AN/SPN-35 aircraft control approach central radar set, and to the right are the forward Mk. 37 director and the navigating bridge. On June 13, 1982, four tugboats moved *Intrepid* to her permanent home at Pier 86 in Manhattan. Almost two hundred former crewmen of the carrier were aboard for that short trip. The formal opening ceremony for the *Intrepid* Sea, Air & Space Museum was August 3, 1982.

On July 4, 1986, *Intrepid* welcomed tourists on the centennial of the unveiling of the Statue of Liberty in New York Harbor. A hot-air balloon promoting US Navy recruiting is tethered to the flight deck.

During Fleet Week in late May 2002, several active-service warships, including one from the Royal Danish Navy, are docked around *Intrepid* (*background*) at the Sea, Air & Space Museum. This was the fifteenth annual Fleet Week, and the first to be held since the September 11, 2001, terrorist attacks.

On December 5, 2006, *Intrepid* was moved from her pier for the first time in twenty-four years, for a nearly two-year period of repairs and refurbishment at Bayonne, New Jersey. The bottom of the hull was encased in muck at the pier, and several attempts had to be made before tugboats freed her. The carrier is seen here opposite the Statue of Liberty on December 5. At Bayonne, the hull would be sandblasted and repainted. Later, *Intrepid* was moved to Staten Island for renovation work on its exhibition spaces.

Intrepid is in drydock at the Bayonne Dry Dock and Repair Corporation, where the carrier has been repainted, on May 28, 2007. Some of the exhibition aircraft on the flight deck have been encased in protective covers. While this renovation work was underway, the ship's home at Pier 86 was being refurbished.

A crewman manning a machine gun on a patrol craft from Coast Guard Station New York is providing security for *Intrepid* as tugboats move the carrier back to Pier 86 in Manhattan following her almost two-year period of repairs and refitting, on October 2, 2008.

Enterprise, perched atop a NASA 747 shuttle carrier aircraft (SCA), is making a pass over the Hudson River, with its new home, the *Intrepid* Sea, Air & Space Museum, directly below, on April 27, 2012. *Enterprise* was NASA's first orbiter in the space shuttle program, serving as an atmospheric test aircraft mated to an SCA, with no engines, heat shield, or certain other systems installed. After landing at JFK International Airport on April 27, *Enterprise* was demated from the SCA and placed on a barge, on which it would be transported to the *Intrepid* Sea, Air & Space Museum on June 6, 2012.

Intrepid is magnificently illuminated by the late-afternoon sun alongside Pier 86 on December 11, 2011. This was a landmark day for the museum ship: a few hours earlier, NASA transferred the title and ownership of the shuttle orbiter *Enterprise* to the *Intrepid* Sea, Air & Space Museum. *Intrepid* would receive *Enterprise*, which at that time was at the National Air and Space Museum's Steven F. Udvar-Hazy Center, during the following spring.

Intrepid is viewed from just above the water in her berth at Pier 86, home of the *Intrepid* Sea, Air & Space Museum. In the foreground are the anchors. The bow anchor has a special fairing, with cutouts for the anchor flukes, and a grooved front to guide the anchor shank into the hawsepipe as it is raised. On the flight deck aft of the island is the aircraft-restoration hangar, aft of which is the space shuttle pavilion, which houses *Enterprise*. Rich Kolasa

In a view of the starboard side of the island, above the black-painted flag bridge is the navigating bridge, over which is the forward Mk. 37 director, with a Mk. 25 fire-control radar on top. On the tripod jutting from the upper starboard side of the island is the AN/SPS-29 air-search radar antenna. On the opposite side of the pole mast is the AN/SPS-30 height-finder antenna. *Rich Kolasa*

The amidships area of *Intrepid* is seen from the starboard side. At the center, between the hangar deck and the flight deck, is the housing for the escalator, which assisted pilots in moving more quickly from the ready rooms belowdecks to the flight deck. *Rich Kolasa*

As seen from the aft-starboard quarter, the smokestack of *Intrepid* has a permanent metal cover on top. To the lower left is the dome for the AN/SPN-35 aircraft control approach central radar antenna. Above it, on the rear of the superstructure, is the primary fly control station, with tinted green windows. PriFly was moved to this location during the 1956–57 modernization. *Rich Kolasa*

Details of the aft part of the starboard side of the island are depicted; the smokestack is to the upper right. The drum-shaped structure with the dish antenna on it, aft of the smokestack, is the foundation for the aft Mk. 37 director; that director was removed from the ship in the mid-1960s. On the upper part of the bulwark, adjacent to the foundation, are a venturi windscreen, which diverted air up and away from the platform, and a bracket for a whip antenna. *Rich Kolasa*

In a continuation of the preceding photo, above the superstructure as seen from the starboard side are, *left to right*, the AN/SPS-29 antenna, the pole mast, and the SPS-30 pencil-beam height-finder radar antenna. Midway up the pole mast is the AN/SPN-6 control-approach antenna. At the top of the pole mast are outriggers, with ECM pods, a TACAN pod, and, *on the right*, an AN/SPS-10 radar antenna. *Rich Kolasa*

Jutting from the starboard side of the upper part of the island is the radar-jamming equipment room. Above that compartment is the tripod that supports the AN/SPS-29 air-search radar antenna. To the right are the forward Mk. 37 director and Mk. 25 fire-control radar antenna and the navigating bridge. *Rich Kolasa*

On the forward part of the island as seen from the starboard side, the black-painted flag bridge juts out more to the front than the navigating bridge one level above. Campaign ribbons are applied to the side of the navigating bridge. To the lower left is the top of the escalator housing, directly above which is the flight deck. *Rich Kolasa*

The flag and navigating bridges are seen from the forward starboard quarter. A catwalk and a handrail are on the outside of the navigating bridge. The flag bridge has a handrail just below the windows, and it used to have a catwalk, but that was removed, probably after the ship was decommissioned, leaving just the stubs of its supports still attached to the bridge. *Rich Kolasa*

The forward starboard 5-inch/38-caliber gun mount is to the left, on the gallery deck. On the same deck, *to the right of center*, is a quadruple 40 mm gun mount; those guns were removed from *Intrepid* in 1953, and this example represents the 40 mm guns on the ship during World War II. *Rich Kolasa*

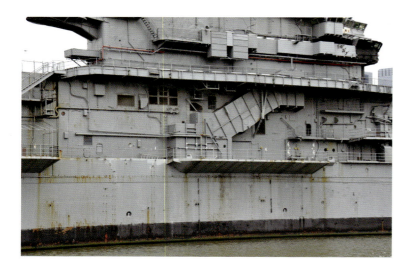

Details of the escalator housing, *center*, as well as of the various platforms, handrails, ladders, vents, and portholes in the starboard amidships area, are displayed. *Rich Kolasa*

Features visible from the starboard side of the bow include the catwalks, the anchors, and the two catapult overruns, the horn-shaped structures at the front of the flight deck. *Rich Kolasa*

As seen from the aft starboard quarter of *Intrepid*, the massive space shuttle pavilion is at the rear of the flight deck, with the smaller aircraft-restoration hangar to the front of it. A tent has been erected on the deck-edge elevator, to the front of which a replica Gemini space capsule and inflatable collar are attached to the hoist cable of the aircraft crane. *Rich Kolasa*

The starboard anchor and the bow anchor are viewed close-up. The bow anchor was installed in 1966, and the port anchor was deleted and its hawsepipe was covered over. The installation of the bow anchor included the addition of a hawsepipe and fairing, shaped to allow the flukes of the anchor to fit snugly in its indentations. *Rich Kolasa*

A section of the gallery deck, the first level below the flight deck, toward the aft part of the port side of *Intrepid*, is depicted, including a catwalk, ladder, and platform. The railings with cyclone fencing along the edge of the flight deck were installed for the safety of visitors to the museum ship. *Rich Kolasa*

This is one of four Mk. 57 Gun Fire Control System (GFCS) directors on *Intrepid*: two were outboard of each side of the flight deck. They were installed in the early 1950s and served to control the 3-inch/50-caliber gun mounts and also could control the 5-inch/38-caliber guns when required. The right side of the director is closest to the camera: on the front of the housing is a Mk. 35 fire-control radar antenna. *Rich Kolasa*

Taken from somewhat forward of the location of the preceding photo, part of the second-from-forward sponson supporting the angled flight deck is seen from below. *Rich Kolasa*

This is the forward sponson that supports the angled flight deck. A small crane is along the forward part of the side of the sponson. To the lower left is the port deck-edge elevator, which has been lowered to the hangar deck. Above the elevator platform are roller doors for a hangar bay. At the upper left is the smokestack. *Rich Kolasa*

The lowered port deck-edge elevator consists of a platform supported by a frame made of pipes. To the left is the forward guide for the elevator. Roller doors are visible on the side of the hangar above the elevator. *Rich Kolasa*

As seen from the pier, at the center in its fully lowered position is the port deck-edge elevator. The curved structure at the front of the elevator, and the matching, curved section of angled flight deck above, formed the leading edge of the angled flight deck when the elevator was raised. Toward the top is the port side of the island, with *Intrepid*'s hull number, 11, on the side of the smokestack. *Rich Kolasa*

As a tribute to *Intrepid*'s role in the early years of the NASA space program, a replica of a Gemini space capsule with a yellow flotation collar deployed around it is suspended from an aircraft crane on the starboard side of *Intrepid. Rich Kolasa*

A 5-inch/38-caliber gun mount on *Intrepid* is viewed from the rear. The mount was equipped with a platform for the crew. On the left rear of the platform is the fuse-setting machine, to the right of which is the breech of the gun. In the background is a quadruple 40 mm gun mount of the type located on *Intrepid* during World War II. *Rich Kolasa*

Throughout *Intrepid*'s career, the 5-inch/38-caliber gun mounts were her most powerful onboard defensive weapons. Termed dual-purpose guns because of their effectiveness against both aircraft and surface targets, these guns were mounted singly, as seen here, or in twin-gun mounts. The single 5-inch guns were on platforms along the gallery deck and had sparse protection for the guns and crews, in the form of splinter shields (*foreground*). *Rich Kolasa*

The matte black paint on the front of the island and the flag bridge replicates a feature that was present on *Intrepid* from around mid-1956 to the end of the ship's operational service. The ship's nickname, "Fighting I," is painted on the front of the island, below the flag bridge, and this replicates a marking that first appeared, on the basis of photographic evidence, in 1968 or possibly slightly earlier. *Rich Kolasa*

Intrepid's campaign ribbons and a round plate with the insignia of the Tonkin Gulf Yacht Club (the nickname of the Seventh Fleet in the Vietnam War) are on the navigating bridge, *to the left*. Farther aft is PriFly, with its tilted and green-tinted windows, below which is a compartment for a television camera and operator, to record flight-deck operations. *Rich Kolasa*

As seen from the forward-port quarter of the island of the museum ship *Intrepid*, the radar and ECM antenna arrays above the island are close in appearance to the arrays in the final years of the carrier's operational service. *Rich Kolasa*

Atop the navigating bridge, as seen from the forward-port quarter of the island, is the Mk. 37 director, with its Mk. 25 dish antenna on a frame above it. Jutting from the side of the director is the left side of the optical rangefinder. The housing for the director was formed of welded ¾-inch armor plate, and it housed six crewmen: the director officer, pointer, and trainer were in the front, and the assistant control officer, rangefinder operator, and radar operator were in the rear. *Rich Kolasa*

The antenna arrays are seen from a slightly closer perspective. One item that is missing is the TACAN antenna's dome-shaped housing, which was present at the center top of the pole mast, between the dome-shaped ECM antennas, in 1975, but had been removed from the mast sometime over the next seven years. *Rich Kolasa*

The navigating bridge incorporates the pilothouse, or primary conning station, to the front and sides of which is an enclosed space with windows around it. Shown here is the aft starboard section of the bridge, where the navigator's chair and his compass repeater are located. This is where the navigator was stationed while the carrier was performing at-sea refueling or UNREP (underway replenishment), since from here the navigator had an unimpeded view of the entire starboard quarter. Toward the left is a speaking tube, through which voice messages could be spoken to lower levels. *Rich Kolasa*

The pilothouse, or primary conning station, is in an enclosed space, with portholes, in the center of the navigating bridge. From here, the ship was maneuvered. To the lower right is the helm, of highly polished brass. To the left of the helm is the engine-order telegraph, a communications device by which instructions for engine speed and direction were transmitted to the engine room. To the front of the helm is the rudder-angle indicator, above which are two compass repeaters. *Rich Kolasa*

Proceeding forward from the navigator's station, the forward starboard corner of the navigating bridge is in view. Plexiglas panels in the foreground are to bar visitors from handling the instruments, which include a radar scope (*center*), compasses, television monitors, and other gear. *Rich Kolasa*

In the forward port corner of the navigating bridge is the captain's chair, to the front of which is a television monitor, which constantly showed activities on the flight deck. To the right of the monitor is a telephone set, through which he could communicate with any department on the carrier. Above the phone is a box with wind-speed and wind-direction indicators. *Rich Kolasa*

The captain's chair and instruments are seen from the rear, with a Plexiglas barrier in the foreground. In addition to the slanted side and front windows, which reduced glare, overhead windows were provided for the bridge. Just out of sight to the left is a large, convex mirror by which the captain could see activities to the rear on the flight deck. *Rich Kolasa*

One level below is the flag bridge, where the admiral who flew his flag from *Intrepid* had his base of operations. Shown here is part of the bridge, with indicators, radar scope, and swiveling chair. Like the navigating bridge, the flag bridge was enclosed during the 1952–53 refurbishment, but the overhead windows were not introduced until later. *Rich Kolasa*

Just a few steps from the navigating bridge is the captain's sea cabin: a spartan compartment where the captain slept when at sea. Furnishings were limited to a rack (bed) with drawers underneath, table, and chair. *Rich Kolasa*